DIARY
OF A
COUNTRY WOMAN

Best Wishes
Peggy Cole

DIARY
OF A
COUNTRY
WOMAN

by
PEGGY COLE

Illustrations by
Tricia Newell

MORROW & CO. PUBLISHERS
BUNGAY · SUFFOLK
1991

Dedication

For all my readers, radio listeners
and visitors to "Akenfield"
over many happy years

First published Morrow & Co., Bungay, Suffolk 1991

ISBN 0 948903 12 0

Typeset by Bungay Printers, 4b Market Place, Bungay
Printed and bound by The Ipswich Book Company

Contents

Acknowledgements

I am most grateful to my dear friend, Iris Stebbings, for editing and typing the manuscript, with help from Cecil Cousins.

Thanks are also accorded to Tricia Newell for her beautiful drawings and to Seley Little for all his valuable advice.

Foreword

THIS BOOK of diary notes represents a year in the life of a remarkable and highly-regarded countrywoman, who lives in one of our loveliest and least-spoilt counties — Suffolk.

Peggy Cole's diary has notes for every day of what was an unforgettable year in her life.

Readers of her two previous books — "A Country Girl at Heart" (Brechinset Publications, 1985) and "Country Cottage Companion" (David & Charles, 1988) and visitors to her famous council-house garden in the remote village of Charsfield (beyond Wickham Market and Woodbridge) will need no introduction to Peggy Cole's passionate and industrious devotion to country life.

Her widowed life-style holds in balance a love of old rural ways, with acceptance of modern amenities and methods. But the creeping urbanisation of the countryside, with theme parks and too many motorways is not for her.

This latest report from Peggy's world is not a dramatic, highly-coloured or racy read. But for those who relish the blessed quiet of the countryside, it offers a gentle progress through her daily round.

These "day-to-day" notes have, in fact, a curiously pleasant monotony, with their details about gardening; preserving; wine-making; writing regular columns for local newspapers; appearances on two weekly radio programmes; lecturing with slides; judging at summer shows and not least of all, babysitting! They also frequently turn up incidents and insights one is pleased to share, and the diary achieves a compelling climax with Peggy's autumn visit to the U.S.A. for her first overseas lecture-tour.

Much of Peggy's gardening and social effort is devoted to charitable ends and a brief note here on how this all began will interest new readers.

Peggy and her farm-worker husband, Ernie Cole, developed their colourful garden more than twenty years ago and in 1970 were asked if they would open it to the public for fund-raising. This soon escalated from occasional openings to becoming a full-time summer attraction. Peggy, meanwhile, was also making a name as an exhibitor at local flower-shows — and eventually she became a leading judge at these events.

In 1972 at such a show, the Suffolk-born theatre and film director, Peter Hall (now Sir Peter), was searching for a possible mother-figure in his ambitious film adaptation of "Akenfield" — Ronald Blythe's celebrated book on rural life in the region over a period of about eighty years. To her astonishment, Peggy was approached and she eventually agreed to tackle the role, in a company mainly composed of local people.

Peggy has subsequently given her slide-show lecture on the making of the film to hundreds of social groups all over East Anglia, and has named her house and garden "Akenfield".

Seley Little

Wivenhoe, Colchester

January

THURSDAY JANUARY 1 — My brother Ronnie and I spent New Year's Day together at my home in the Suffolk village of Charsfield and today, I bet that nobody else was doing the same as us! Ronnie works for the local council and has a small bungalow in the village but spends much of his spare time helping me — he was sorting out all my home-made wine corks, labels and other related items. He also made lots of labels out of old pieces of plain cardboard. I sorted out all my jam jars, matching up lids, as they will be useful later in the year. I make a lot of jams for local W.I. markets and it is practical to have the standard-size jars. I also racked five gallons of dried fruit wine, and am hoping that this will turn out like sherry.

The weather has been very mild today. I am going to have an early night as I was baby-sitting for the family at Melton last night.

Friday January 2 — Did a lot of wine racking today. I started with Fig and Date, which doubtless some of my visitors will think is a good laxative; then I made two gallons of Parsnip, using the base of the dried fruit from yesterday for this wine; it seemed such a waste to throw all the dried fruit away.

Went to Woodbridge to do some shopping for the week-end, then went on to Ipswich to do my first Gardening Hour programme on Radio Orwell for 1987.

Saturday January 3 — Weather still very mild. Did a lot of tidying up in my greenhouse, checking over pot plants for signs of mildew. My plastic lining is very good, but I do get a lot of condensation. I try to open doors and windows whenever possible.

Two friends, Iris and Claude Stebbings of Wickham Market, came to stay for the week-end and, during the evening, I showed them slides of the many photos taken of the garden and village over the past year — we had four hours of viewing.

Sunday January 4 — We all sat and had an easy day. Needless to say, it was pouring with rain by lunchtime. I even managed to get my brother to sit and have a rest, and I cannot remember when he last sat down for so long! Claude brought some tasty Peach wine and we sampled my Rosehip. We also sampled Sloe gin which I had made in the previous October. It was a very enjoyable week-end and we had a lot of good chat about wines and exchanged ideas on blending.

Monday January 5 — A nice bright day. Some American visitors called to see whether I could help them trace a family tree. They had relations living in the village many years ago but unfortunately, I could not help them a lot so I suggested that they go to see Uncle George at Dallinghoo, who might be able to give them a lead.

At lunchtime, I went babysitting and looked after Russell and Sarah, my eldest son Allan's children. I took them for a walk at Melton to feed the ducks but the wind was so cold, we did not stay out long. In the evening, there was the first Parish Council meeting of the new year. Planning permission was being sought for a recreation facility behind South View, since building permission had been turned down for any more houses.

Tuesday January 6 — I planted first seeds of lettuce, All-year-round, Golden Acre cabbage and also Cauliflower, Leeks and Red Cabbage. I also started Begonia tubers in my propagator. The day was rather windy and chilly, but a friend and her husband, Margaret and Alan Bradley, called; she used to be my nursing Sister when I worked at St. Audrey's Psychiatric Hospital. They took me out to lunch at the local pub, The Three Horseshoes, for lunch. This was all very pleasant — I must say that our pub does excellent meals. After they left, I went and bought a hundredweight of potatoes from a local farmer, for £2.75.

Wednesday January 7 — Sorted out my preserves today, ready for the W.I. Market at Woodbridge, then I went and did my "Peggy's Patch" on Radio Orwell. It is a pity that I am now on in the afternoons rather than the mornings, as I lose quite a lot of time over this otherwise enjoyable engagement. Later, I sorted out my Bramley apples, they have not kept so well this winter, many of them have gone very spotted with "bitter pip" but at least the birds like them.

Thursday January 8 — Went to the W.I. Market at Woodbridge to take my jams and pickles. I have not started to take leeks or parsnips yet. I bought a first lot of Seville oranges, 6lb at 30p per lb.

I racked my parnsip wine and also made two gallons of orange wine, using the remaining oranges from Christmas, and made it from pure orange juice. This is an experiment but I thought it would make a nice wine.

Friday January 9 — Weather changing today, bringing cold winds. I notice that the birds have come to the table much more, so I think we are in for a cold spell. I also made twenty pounds of marmalade, went and did my second gardening programme of the week at Radio Orwell, after which I was glad to get home in the warm. I am so pleased with my Parkray fire — how people manage without open fires now, I don't know, but maybe I am old-fashioned.

Saturday January 10 — Wind still very cold. I walked around the garden to see what needed to be protected in the shrubs, I wrapped my Fatsia up, also Solanum Crispum and variegated Lavatera. The latter was so pretty last year and it has made a big shrub, I don't want to lose it. Ronnie brought me some logs which he had cut from an old tree and we put these in my toolshed because I think snow is on the way. I also sorted my seeds out to plant. Went babysitting for my son Allan and daughter-in-law Jackie, at Melton. I left their home at 1.15 in the morning and had one of the worst drives home in an awful snowstorm, at times it was difficult to see to drive. It took me nearly three-quarters of an hour to travel from Melton to Charsfield, which is only a distance of about six miles.

Sunday January 11 — Bad weather set in, snowing very hard. Ronnie was called out early by the Council to grit up. I cannot remember when it snowed so hard. I didn't venture out to church. The only creature pleased to see the snow, I think, was my little dog Sally. She keeps watching me to see whether I am going to put my coat on and take her out. I have heard it said many times, that dogs seem to like the snow. I watched from my window as the shimmering flakes fell down and saw the birds trying to get under the hedge for shelter. Needless to say, I never had any visitors, few cars were around and those out were moving very slowly indeed.

Monday January 12 — In all my twenty-six years of living here, I have never seen so much snow or felt the cold so keenly. The wastepipe from my kitchen sink is frozen solid and I am having to throw my dirty water down the toilet. The poor birds are looking for food and I am glad that I kept my spotty apples. I also made some bird cake, as I call it, by warming some fat and then putting bread, stale cake and any bits and pieces into it. This goes into a basin, then when cool, I turn it out on the bird table. As fast as I put water out, it freezes hard!

Tuesday January 13 — Many parts of Suffolk are now cut off. The Government have announced that they will give the old people five pounds this week, for heating. I reckon that they should have put it up to twenty pounds, it hardly buys one bag of coal. The wind is getting up and the snow is drifting. I walked into my greenhouse and noticed my onions, which I had planted on Boxing Day, need pricking out, but I shall bring my compost pots etc, in the house where it is warmer. It is best to keep greenhouse doors tightly closed, with this cold wind about. As fast as you sweep the path, the wind brings the snow all back again.

Wednesday January 14 — I turned my radio on at 6.00 am. Police said Suffolk and Essex are at a standstill, winds in the night having cut whole communities off with drifting snow. By God! that east wind is now on my back door, I have even laid old coats down to keep the icy blasts out.

My poor old chickens — I have been feeding them in the hut because the snow is too deep for them to walk around outside and I am surprised that I am still getting eggs from them. My brother dug a wide path for me last night so that I could get up to feed them. I have never before experienced trying to dig myself out from the greenhouse to the chicken hut.

Later, I made four loaves of bread and some cakes — thank God for a freezer, I say, in this weather! Living in the country it is always best to keep an extra bag of flour by you, in the winter months.

Thursday January 15 — Howling winds all night. This has blown all the snow on to the roads. Police warned, on the radio, that it is much worse than yesterday as roads are now blocked in many more places and advised people to stay indoors. Ronnie and his mates have been out with the local farmer, a tractor and a digger, trying to clear the Street. This is where local radio is so helpful, telling people where to get bread and milk etc. We have had no fresh milk since Monday, no post or papers.

The snow was four foot high near my chicken run this morning. The village has been very quiet today as no cars are out, only the roaring tractor and the council men digging and moving snow. I should think that they must be exhausted — and the police as well.

I have never seen so many birds flocking at the bird table, even pigeons. But looking on the brighter side, my bowl of blue hyacinths have given me a lot of pleasure. Thank goodness, we have now got the telephone; it means a lot to be able to talk to neighbours and to offer help. I do feel sorry for the old people: in the villages we keep an eye on all the old and ill people and help them where we can.

Friday January 16 — I managed to prick out my onions today, but I have put them in the back bedroom. I also managed to walk up the lane and take lots of photos of the snow. Winds have died down in the night and most of the "A" roads were open by lunchtime, but still a lot of villages are cut off. Mr. Kitson, our local farmer, organised milk for the village, a treat, as we have had no deliveries since Monday.

Hooray! the postman came at lunchtime. All I want now is my old *East Anglian* and I shall be happy. It is surprising how we miss the little pleasures of life. My gardening programme on Radio Orwell has had to be cancelled this week — the first time in my six years with the station.

Saturday January 17 — What a relief, a thaw has set in! Still, some roads remain blocked in the village. I managed to get my car out and went to Woodbridge, but found room only for one-way traffic. Driving was very treacherous in places. I bought myself a pair of snow boots.

I have never seen such long icicles hanging from my greenhouses. The chickens ventured out for the first time today and we even had papers and milk delivered once more.

My brother Ronnie is looking very tired; he is like the rest of the Council men, they have had a hard week working most of the time from 4.30 am to 6.00 pm, with scarcely any break.

Sunday January 18 — Letheringham and Hoo villages are still cut off, so I cannot get through to the early service in the lovely old church at Hoo. I had some coal delivered this morning, the first time I have known the coalman to come on a Sunday, with a tractor and trailer! Ronnie knocked the snow off my chicken run as it was so heavy and was pulling the wire down. I sat and did a lot of my correspondence from Christmas and just had an easy day.

Monday January 19 — Today the thaw has started in earnest and the snow diggers are making the roads a bit wider. People are going back to work after being shut up in their homes all the week. I drove to Melton to look after the grandchildren, Russell $3^1/_2$ years and Sarah nearly 2. It is remarkable how much they love you to play and read to them. They are still young and innocent and it is lovely to see them so happy. Russell surprised me this afternoon by saying his alphabet right the way through.

Tuesday January 20 — I walked up to the village today to see the Rev. and Mrs. Laurie and took more photos of the snow around the village. Later I racked my gooseberry wine and sorted out other wines. My fruit wine seems to have stopped working so I will have to try a few more tricks with it — perhaps add a little more yeast.

Weather has been very dull today. The air seems warmer and there is no sign of frost. I am surprised that my chickens are still laying so well.

Wednesday January 21 — Woke up to rather thick fog. I went to Ipswich to do my radio programme. Also made some Suffolk rusks and flapjacks. I was very pleased with the slides of the snow scenes which I had taken — this is a nice way to keep a little bit of history, and I am sure that many people will enjoy seeing them as I use them with my lectures around the country. We can actually see the grass once more, the snow going very quickly now.

Thursday January 22 — I went to London today to do a programme for the British Forces Broadcasting Service for Over-seas Forces. I enjoyed the day but there is nothing like coming home to dear old Suffolk. How people live in those high-rise flats I will never know. I had to cancel going to the Horticultural Club's Annual Dinner at Capel St. Mary as it was too foggy to drive.

Friday January 23 — A mild day for the middle of winter. Mrs. Hope-Thorpe brought me a lovely bunch of chrysanthemums and it was very pleasant as I took her around the garden. We looked at the buds peeping out after the snow and even saw some primroses coming through. After lunch I went to the local farm and bought potatoes and a box of Jonagold apples; they really are a nice crisp apple. This evening I have been to Ipswich to do my gardening programme on Radio Orwell.

Saturday January 24 — A nice bright day and still mild weather. I went to the local gardening centre at Notcutts in Woodbridge and spent my Christmas garden voucher on some Gloxinia corms, I also bought two tubers of Gloriosa Rothschildiana. Came home and started these off in my propagator and also pricked out four trays of various cabbage and lettuce seedlings. Finished the day by doing a lot of writing and sorting out material for my next book.

Sunday January 25 — Went to church at Hoo at 8.30 am then had a walk around the garden to see whether the snow has done any damage with its weight on the shrubs. I am sure that people don't realise how heavy snow can be and what a lot of damage it can do if it is not knocked off shrubs and bushes. The little clump of Cedric Morris narcissi which my friend Beth Chatto from Elmstead gave me has brought so much pleasure, with their small yellow heads — they are like small jewels. They have been in bloom since October and are still going strong. During the day,

I have planted some geranium seeds and popped these into the propagator. Ronnie dug up the rest of the sprout land and split a lot of kindling wood for me.

Monday January 26 — Saw my first snowdrops in the garden today. Weather not too cold for the time of the year but in the country, we often say it is a "weather-breeder", meaning that there is more cold to come. I went to Wivenhoe near Colchester to see Beth Chatto's brother, Seley Little, as he is going to look at the finished manuscript for my second book. Seley has a dear little town garden and many people would be surprised to see what can be done with such a small patch. Beth and Seley have designed this for easy maintenance, and have some interesting "before and after" photographs. It is important, I feel, to take photos before you start to design a garden and then you can see what you have achieved after it is all finished.

Tuesday January 27 — I still can't believe that it is so mild. I let my chickens run out today in the orchard belonging to my neighbour, Mr. Alan Spicer, who is very kind and lets them wander about in there so that they can have some fresh grass.

I notice the shrubs are rather advanced and I do hope that we shall not get too many hard frosts as this will set them back.

I racked my fruit wine again; I think it is working better now. David, my younger son, came to visit today and I was able to give him what I call a Red Cross parcel of leeks, brussels-sprouts, carrots, marmalade, jam and some eggs. David, like Allan, is with the Suffolk Police and his wife Norine is a nurse at Heath Road Hospital, Ipswich.

Wednesday January 28 — I went to Ipswich this morning and did my "Peggy's Patch" broadcast; came home and made a chocolate cake. I also put the labels on my jars of preserves for the W.I. market tomorrow. We had some sad news today on the radio — Terry Waite, the Archbishop's special envoy was reported missing after a week in Lebanon. I hope he is safe; he is a very good man and he has helped many people, both in this country and abroad.

Thursday January 29 — Very sharp frost this morning, but by ten o'clock, the sun had come out and it was a lovely day. I went out and helped at the W.I. market in Woodbridge; I am amazed at how the people stand and queue, waiting for the door to open, but I can understand it if they live on their own or perhaps have visitors coming for the week-end, because they can buy items in small quantities or even order a special cake or pie to be made.

When I got home, I opened my greenhouse doors and it was lovely to feel the air circulating through. The sun is gaining more power so a lot of my pot plants need watering. I even managed to pot up some of my ivy geranium cuttings which had over-wintered in old tomato trays.

Friday January 30 — A nice bright day after the frost cleared, so have had a "blitz'"on my sheds at the top of the garden, tidying up all my seed trays and flower pots. Have had some parsnips stored in an old bath but I think a rat or rabbit has been after them so I think it is much better if they are left in a clamp in the garden. My Hoya plant has the mealy bug all over it so have had to paint it with methylated spirits. This is a nasty little insect and you can detect it as it leaves a white mould everywhere. Since the plant is a large one, the treatment took a long while to do.

Saturday January 31 — Very cold day but nice and bright, just what you expect for January. I cut up 8lb of oranges for marmalade while my brother Ronnie cleaned out my chicken house and did some tidying up around the woodshed. Took my little dog, Sally, for a walk round the orchard and she caught two rabbits. Poor things, they have got this awful disease, myxomatosis. This is a virus which kills rabbits, and I am afraid, has put country people off eating them.

This evening, have been to our local church supper at the

Charsfield Village Hall — it was very good, with a four-course meal and coffee for £2.50, very cheap as prices go these days. The village people provided a most enjoyable evening of entertainment.

I think we shall remember January 1987 for one of the coldest spells ever on record. The snow began to fall on the 6th of the month and for seventeen days Suffolk and Essex had a taste of real winter weather; a total of nine inches of snow fell. January 12th was the coldest day of the century with 16 degrees of frost in many places.

HINTS FOR JANUARY

MY first tip — make a New Year's resolution to keep a diary or a notebook, with dates recorded for sowing seeds, planting, pricking out, potting up, feeding, flowering, pest diseases, etc. — you will find this so useful in the months ahead. A lot of gardening can be done indoors this month, sitting by the fireside with the seed catalogues spread over the table. Plans can be made for the coming year but do get the seed orders off early to avoid disappointment.

One job I like to do in January is to give all my gardening tools a good clean and rub them down with oily rags. Seed pans and trays should be washed with Jeyes Fluid and you can start to sow a pinch of cabbage seed, Hispi Primo, also lettuce. I like to sow the red cabbage seed at the end of this month so that I get good plants to set out in April. We often get severe weather now so if the heat is down in the greenhouse, cover plants temporarily with newspapers, but remember not to leave them on longer than necessary since plants do need light as well as warmth. If, like me, you save your own pea and bean seed, don't leave them in a plastic container. I made the mistake of doing this and the mice ate through the plastic container and ate the seed as well. If you have a few shallots left over, put about six or seven in a pot and place them on the kitchen windowsill, you will have nice green shoots for early salads.

I like to cut some forsythia and bring it indoors. Placed in water in a warm room, the flowers will soon show, even the green leaves help to brighten up a dull day. If you were lucky enough to have been given azaleas, cyclamen, cineraria or poinsettia as Christmas presents, there are certain points to remember. Firstly, never let the frost touch them and never over-water them, except for azaleas. Wait until the compost feels dry before standing them in a bowl of water until the top of the compost is moist, then drain and put them back into position. Keep the compost of azaleas slightly moist all the time during flowering. Neither azaleas or cyclamen need a high temperature, 50°F is ideal, whilst poinsettia prefer it slightly warmer at 55°F.

Another task which can be undertaken, sitting down indoors, is to collect garden labels for cleaning, which can be done with a Brillo pad. If you have to go round the garden to find these, be careful not to walk on the lawn during frost weather as this can damage the grass — it could turn black and suffer all the summer.

In snowy weather, shake the snow off the trees and shrubs, especially conifers, as it can pull the branches down and even break them, permanently spoiling their shape.

CARROT WHISKY
(A good social wine)

Ingredients

$^1/_2$lb wheat
4lb carrots
$2^1/_2$lb sugar
$^1/_2$ pint grape concentrate (white)
$^1/_2$ level teaspoon grape tannin
1 level teaspoon citric acid
1 level teaspoon tartaric acid
1 level teaspoon pectic enzyme

Wash the wheat and soak it overnight in 1 pint cold water to soften it. Next day, strain and discard the liquid. Scrub the carrots, cut them into slices and cook them in 5 pints water until they are soft (do not allow them to mash up). Straining the liquor from the carrots, pour it onto sugar, acids, tannin and soft wheat. Stir until sugar has dissolved and allow to cool. When the temperature is at 70°F (21°C) add the pectic enzyme, cover and leave overnight. Next day, make up to $7^1/_2$ pints with warm water, add yeast starter and ferment for 7 days in a covered bucket, stirring daily. After 7 days, transfer to a demijohn and seal with an airlock, adding the grape concentrate at this time. Ferment out to finish.

This wine can be very potent.

February

SUNDAY FEBRUARY 1 — February has started off very cold, with 10 degrees of frost. I made a lot of marmalade, also made some orange and wheat wine and spent quite a long time talking to the family on the telephone — what a boon this little unit is for all of us! On the whole I have had an easier day.

There is still no news of Terry Waite.

Monday February 2 — Still cutting up oranges for marmalade, but now I find I am running short of jam jars. The frost has lifted a bit today; walking around the garden, have noticed my Arum, Italicum Pictum looking very bright against the snow, the veined leaves are so pretty. It is nice to have a bit of foliage showing.

Spent the afternoon looking after the grandchildren so I took along some of my old slides and gave them a little film show of a collection of animals which I had taken over the years. The children were very good and sat still; it is amazing how interested they were. Later, we went for a walk around the playing field at Melton.

Tuesday February 3 — Very foggy this morning. I went to a W.I. Committee meeting in Ipswich then did a little shopping. I heard a rumour today that the local radio station — Radio Orwell — is being taken over by Radio Broadland but don't know if there is any truth in this.

I had two magpies in the garden today; there are so many of

these birds about these days and yet a few years ago, you hardly saw any.

I noticed rats had been at one of my parsnips which were stored in an old wheelbarrow. How they got it off the wheelbarrow I can't think, they had even tried to pull it down a hole.

Wednesday February 4 — Another day of fog. I do hate driving in this weather but went to Ipswich and did my programme. There is still a lot of snow around the country roads and single-lane traffic in some places. As I took my dog, Sally, for a walk this afternoon I noticed the wild arum leaves coming up also the large rabbit holes in the banks. The mother (doe) rabbit will soon be looking for a place to have her young; you can usually tell, for they make a much bigger hole than the usual burrow.

Thursday February 5 — A much better day. I went to the W.I. market this morning, taking marmalade. It was a bigger than usual market today, as people could come in from the country after the bad weather and a lot more cakes and produce were on sale. I had a good afternoon tidying up plants in the greenhouse, some needed a little more water now as they start to shoot. Hopefully, I shall soon be able to take some cuttings off my fuschias. Tonight I went to the Co-op Gardening Club at Ipswich, to appear on their quiz so I was a bit late getting home.

Friday February 6 — I hope it is not a weather-breeder today as the sun came out and it was just like a Spring day. My friend Sheila Woods and her husband, Dick, who live at Bredfield, about four miles away from me, took me out to Easton White Horse for lunch, as a present for my birthday. It was lovely to visit my old place of birth and it is such a pretty village. Later in the day I washed the car and I thought how nice it was to be outside. I also noticed today that the gorse has a few flowers coming out — there is an old saying, "If the gorse has flowers on it at Valentines, you can kiss your loved one".

Saturday February 7 — I spent the morning clearing out my small shed — this is where I keep all my flower arranging bits and pieces. A rat had got in and done a lot of damage — eaten a hole through the floor, in fact! I even managed to open the green-house doors today, and a robin and blackbird were outside singing to their heart's content. Tonight my brother Ronnie and some other friends took me out for my birthday, we went to the Falcon at Earl Soham. Going out for meals two days running — I shall have to start thinking about a diet again!!

Sunday February 8 — What a change in the weather today, with the rain. I always did say take each day as it comes and enjoy it; such a difference from yesterday. I went to early service at Hoo Church, it was lovely to see the first daffodils and helibores on the altar. My friend, Perry Branton who lives at Hoo, has a son who is getting married at Easter so, after the service, we sat planning the church flowers. I also noticed today the catkins, or lamb's tails as we call them, were all out, a welcome sign that Spring is on the way.

Monday February 9 — Another wet morning but it soon brightened up. We have a saying "if it rains before seven it will clear up before eleven". I went to see the Rev. Laurie in the morning, about the Charsfield Church meeting and plans for the Church fete. He has a fairly busy life, looking after the six parishes of Charsfield with Debach, Hoo, Letheringham, Monewden and Dallinghoo. Then I took Sally for a walk around the orchard and was amazed when I saw all the tree prunings lying on the ground, how the rabbits have eaten them almost bare. It just shows what damage they can do to growing trees.

In the evening I went to the W.I. meeting, it was interesting as we had a local man talking about Francis Light who lived in Dallinghoo in the 1700's and who, after being educated at Seckford Grammar School in Woodbridge, joined the Navy. After leaving the Service, he worked for the East India Company at Madras. Learning the native languages, he travelled to Malaya, where he established a trading post for the Company. Occupying the island of Penang in the name of King George III, he raised the British flag on 11th August 1786. This colonial pioneer died in 1799 of malaria and was buried in Penang where a statue stands to his memory.

Tuesday February 10 — Went to Ipswich to record my radio programme for tomorrow, did some shopping and bought 8lb of oranges, 2lb for 25p, so this was good value. I also had four eggs today from my chickens, they are looking very well and have enjoyed being let out into the orchard each day. Tonight I went to Bradfield near Harwich to show my "Akenfield" slides at the W.I. (Thank goodness the weather was kind for driving). I must add here that these slide pictures are not of my house and gardens which are called "Akenfield", but are a record of the making of the 1974 film version of Ronald Blythe's famous book of the same name, with which I was involved with all my family.

Ronald's book, which he wrote in 1967 while living in Charsfield, is an account of village life in this part of Suffolk over a period of about eighty years, starting in the late Victorian era. Sir Peter Hall directed this film, with a cast of local people instead of professional actors. He chose me to play the role of the mother and Ronald appeared as the vicar in the unforgettable funeral scene. Ernie, my husband, helped with the ploughing scenes and was one of several people who found authentic period items for various sequences.

Wednesday February 11 — I was about early this morning as I had to go and look after Sarah (Russell had an appointment at the hospital). Each week I notice new little words and ways of Sarah and one of her favourite tricks is to go through my handbag; she loves to sort out my purse. It was lovely walking up the lane at home today and to hear the birds singing. In the afternoon I went to Easton to show my "Akenfield" slides to the Over 60's Club, then at night I went to Holbrook to the W.I. and gave a talk on gardening. I had a foggy ride home, it was very thick in places and I was thankful to get back safely.

Thursday February 12 — Went to W.I. market in Woodbridge, taking some parsnips and pots of marmalade. Came home and started to plant bedding seeds — salvia, lobelia, statice, rudbeckia, sweet peas, etc. In the evening I went off to lecture at Burstall W.I. on gardening. It has been a busy week with lectures, and apart from last night, the weather has been kind.

Friday February 13 — A nice bright day. I had a morning checking round the greenhouse for mildew. Found a pigeon on my step, looking very poorly, I don't know what is wrong but maybe it has had some poison. Had my hair set today, then I did my gardening notes for the radio. Packed my case ready for going away to Norfolk for the week-end. Sally, my little dog, followed me around, she knows I am going out as soon as I put my different clothes on. Returning from doing my programme in Ipswich, I was picked up by my friends Ruby and Pat Welton and taken to Wymondham.

Saturday February 14 — The weather is not very nice, pouring with rain, but this duly cleared up by eleven o'clock, confirming the old saying. My Friends took me to Norwich where we started off by visiting the Castle Museum (it always strikes me how people years ago built these lovely buildings without the modern tools which man has today). Anyway, back to the Museum — it was very interesting wandering around, I would have loved to spend the whole day there. An ideal place I thought to take Russell and Sarah when they get a little older. Ted Ellis, who died in July last year (1986), was a wonderful Norfolk naturalist and conservationist and I noticed that he helped to design some of the nature scenes. I hope that one day, a corner of the Museum is set up in his memory.

We visited the famous Colman's Mustard Shop, St. Peter

Mancroft Church then the Cathedral. As one walks in, a feeling of peace is all around in this fine building. We had a nice cup of tea in the Cathedral teashop and as we left by the south door I noticed Edith Cavell's grave. I also took a photograph of her statue. On the way back to Wymondham we drove via Cringleford and Ketteringham, past the Lotus factory at Hethel.

Sunday February 15 — I was awakened by the blackbirds singing their heads off. My friend, Ruby, took me to the Holy Communion service at Wymondham Abbey, and what a beautiful abbey it is. I could not forget the altar screen, I don't think I have ever seen a finer one. I am told that this lovely screen is a memorial to the Wymondham men who fell in the First World War. After the service I walked around taking photographs (in bright sunlight and with blue skies). The two towers of this fine abbey must be a landmark for miles around. I was also shown the oldest pub — "Ye Olde Green Dragon Inn", dating from the late fifteenth century and which, I am told, is the best preserved building in the town. It still has scorched timbers from the time when it narrowly escaped the Great Fire of Wymondham in 1615. We also stopped to look at the Market Cross. The original was burned down in the fire but was replaced in 1863 and I am told that only three of this type of building exist in England. A form of a small octagonal Market Hall opens at the ground floor, with a room above. It is a fine example of half-timbered work and is now scheduled as an Ancient Monument.

After an early lunch, Ruby and her husband Pat, took me to see some of Norfolk's coastline. Starting out, they pointed to Ketts Oak, a gnarled shored-up oak tree. Robert Kett and his followers met at this tree to march to Norwich to stage a rebellion against the government (it is worth reading the history of Robert Kett and his brother). We arrived at Cromer and walked along the front, but it was so cold we did not stop for long. Cromer has a nice sandy beach. As we continued along the coast I saw a delightful old windmill at Weybourne also people hang-gliding off the hills.

The nearer we approached to Blakeney, the clouds started to form and snow began to fall. We called in at a charming tea-room to have tea. We saw lots of ducks and geese, and I can understand why birdwatchers come to this part of the country. My mind went again to Ted Ellis as I got out of the car, I remembered how he used to appear on television and tell his stories about the birdlife at Blakeney Point. On our journey, Pat called in and bought some shrimps from a dear little cottage in Salthouse. Our next stop was at Walsingham Abbey and here the snow was falling heavily. We got out of the car and looked around the little abbey and at the courtyard where all the visitors march to on Good Friday. I saw a notice board with all the miles marked on it, from towns where pilgrims come from to see "Our Lady of Walsingham". As the light was fading, we made our way back to Wymondham by Fakenham and East Dereham.

What a lovely week-end; seeing a bit of Norfolk's history and even finishing up with a supper of shrimps and cockle salad.

I arrived home at 9.15 pm, tired but contented and was welcomed by a very pleased little dog, looked after in my absence by Ronnie.

Monday February 16 — I am feeling rather tired today, due to all my gadding about over the week-end, I expect. Sally is behind me wherever I go this morning, she thinks I may go off again. I sorted my mail, did my washing and then went to look after the grandchildren. We went for a walk round Melton to feed the ducks but it snowed on and off so we soon returned home. Had a lazy evening, for a change.

Tuesday February 17 — Off to Ipswich to record "Peggy's Patch", then called in to see a lady who had an orange tree with over seventy oranges on it — it really was a picture. I think she was thrilled to tell me all about it. It all started from her growing a small pip. She also gave me some beans to see if I could tell her the variety. I do have some strange jobs to do since I have been on the radio but it is nice to meet the people and I try to help where I can. I have noticed the rooks flying around today, this may be a good sign, they are looking for their nesting homes.

Wednesday February 18 — A cold day. I left home at 8.00 am to go to London for an I.C.I. Press Day held in the Sugar Room, The Brewery, Chiswell Street. Would you believe it, the train broke down at Stowmarket so all trains running $1^1/_2$ to 2 hours late. Arrived in London at 11.45 am, for meeting about new chemicals for use in gardens etc. Sat next to Peter Seabrook, well-known TV broadcaster and gardening correspondent — had a super lunch. Got home to Charsfield at a quarter past five. After tea, went to Melton to give a talk on "Showing vegetables and preparing for shows".

Thursday February 19 — What a start to the day — my electricity kept going off! A friend came out and found the wire on the side of the house was shorting — this was the wire attached to my greenhouse. After this was fixed, I cut up a lot more oranges for marmalade.

We had some very heavy snow showers today but my telephone has rung non-stop, mainly people ringing up to arrange visits to the garden later in the year.

Friday February 20 — Was very cold today, the wind has moved to the east. I finished cutting up my oranges and also had a visit from a lady coming to do a write-up on myself and the garden, for the *Deben Journal*. My neighbour asked me to go round and kill a rabbit in her garden; the poor old thing had a head as big as a pudding basin, from the dreaded myxomatosis disease, it is only kindness to put such victims out of their misery. I did my usual monthly write-up for the W.I. newspaper, then I went to Ipswich to do the gardening programme.

Saturday February 21 — My latest slides came back today and I was pleased with the ones I took in Norfolk. They included some super views of Wymondham Church. Had one of my bad headaches today and felt I was starting a cold but I managed to make up the rest of my marmalade — 26lb.

I also had a friend come to fit me a loft ladder, it will be very handy and I shall now be able to get up there and store cases and boxes. My sons tell me I store far too much, but I suppose I am old-fashioned and don't like to throw things away.

The weather is still cold but the snowdrops look lovely with their little heads nodding in the wind. I have noticed the nights are pulling out and it is light until after 5.00 pm. I went over to Allan and Jackie's after tea to show them my new slides — the children love to see Grandma's pictures, as they call them.

Sunday February 22 — I still have a heavy cold but I went to my favourite little church at Hoo for early Communion service. I then came home and got out my compost and seeds and had a lovely day sitting at the table sowing them all. I bet there are not many people who bring soil and trays into their sitting room to sow their seeds! After I had planted them all I put them in my propagator. I also pricked out geranium seedlings then I took a walk around the garden as I wanted to take a picture of my Contorta Corkscrew hazel. This is really a picture, with its catkins reaching up to five inches in length but I do wish the birds would leave them on the tree — they are so destructive.

My neighbour, Mr. Spicer, brought me a rabbit which he had shot in his orchard. It is a nice healthy one so I shall skin and cook it.

Monday February 23 — Felt rotten when I got up owing to my developing cold, but it is understandable with this type of weather. I went to the local saleyard as I saw they were advertising a fridge in their sale today. I left a bid, came home and put a lot of boxes etc, in my loft but had to give up later in the day, as my head ached so much. I sat by the fire and cleaned all my plastic gardening labels with a Brillo soap pad, then had an early night.

Tuesday February 24 — My head cold and chest still make me feel down in the dumps. I had a phone call from the saleyard and they told me that I had got my fridge, only ten pounds and just three years old so I was quite pleased with this buy. My old one packed up last week and it is surprising how one misses this modern blessing. I often think how my poor old Mum used to manage with a wooden safe with wire mesh sides. No ice-boxes or fridges for her! We are so lucky, with all our mod-cons of today. I had to kill another rabbit today, Sally was trying to get at it behind my chicken-run. The poor thing was so blind that it couldn't see where it was going. Today, I had a letter from America asking me to fly out in October to start a lecture tour which has been arranged by Patsy Hovenden, President of the Pittsburg Garden Society.

Wednesday February 25 — I went to Ipswich and did my gardening programme then stopped on the way home and picked a few hazel catkins. I love to see them in a vase. I treated myself to a cordless telephone, it will be so handy when I am working outside. Tonight I have done a lot of labels for my wine.

Thursday February 26 — Went and helped at the W.I. market in Woodbridge; took parsnips, strawberry jam, blackberry and apple jelly. We had a very packed market today. After lunch I got into my greenhouse and pricked out pansies and hesperis (sweet rocket). This old-fashioned flower is not often seen in gardens today, but it has a lovely perfume which is very strong, especially at evening time. By late afternoon the rain which started earlier was coming down hard.

Two ladies rang me today about coach parties visiting the garden. I also had a telephone call from another lady who is writing a book and who would like to come and interview me with a view to including my garden in her book, which should be out in the Spring of 1989.

Friday February 27 — I racked a lot of last year's wine this

morning and really had a busy time in the old wine shed. It is
surprising how it gets hold of you when you start to sample it to
see whether it is sweet or dry! I also had a telephone call from a
local paper asking me to write about country life — 500 words a
week — this was a nice surprise. This afternoon I went and gave
my talk on "Akenfield" to the Ipswich Co-op Over 60's Club
then I went on to do my gardening programme for Radio Orwell.

Saturday February 28 — This month is going out with glorious
sunshine — it really was bright and warm in the car today. After
lunch I went to see my Uncle Morry and Aunt Lizzie at
Saxmundham. Uncle is now over eighty and very ill and Aunt
Lizzie, who is eighty-four, does a wonderful job looking after him
as he is in bed most of the time. Despite this, they are a very happy
couple but I really don't know how she manages to look after him.

I came home and did my first write-up for the Woodbridge
Deben Journal, filled some more seed trays with compost ready for
pricking out seedlings. George and Hilda, my step-brother and
his wife, came for supper; I cooked a chicken and was able to pick
herbs from the garden to use as stuffing. Then, after supper, I gave
them a slide show of local events which had taken place during
the past year.

HINTS FOR FEBRUARY

February is often written off on the gardener's calendar, as the weather can be poor and yet, sometimes, conditions can be suitable for some early work outdoors. Particularly towards the end of the month, if conditions allow and the soil is workable, prepare the tilth and sow parsnips. I sow radish seed with my parsnips because these will come up first so that hoeing may be done in between the rows — parsnip seed can take up to six weeks to germinate.

In the greenhouse, box up dahlia tubers, ready to start into growth if you can maintain a temperature of 60°F. Use moist peat or, as I do, the compost from old grow-bags. The dahlias will produce strong shoots from which cuttings can be taken, at about 3 inches in length.

Seed potatoes can be bought now, taken from the net bags and put into chitting trays (old egg trays are excellent for this purpose). Store in a light, frost-free place.

Start to sow seeds for bedding plants such as antirrhinums, begonias, lobelias, ageratums, and impatiens (busy lizzies). So many ask me why they are unable to get impatiens to germinate well and one of the reasons is that they do need extra warmth, up to 70°F. However, one good thing I have found, is that in my greenhouse, when I stand my impatiens on the top shelf for the summer, their seed falls down onto the gravel on the bottom shelf, and I have small seedlings popping up all over the shelf — these I can then prick out into trays. Early begonias, gloxinias and achimenes (hot water plant) can also be started into growth this month.

To get the best from your rhubarb, it needs to be covered with straw and an old dustbin or tin bath — this will help it to produce those early red sticks.

You will notice that the clematis are beginning to show signs of activity so now is the time to prune them back to within about two inches of the ground. This may seem pretty drastic treatment as it means cutting away a lot of buds further up the plant but you will find that it grows better and flowers more freely. I must point out, and it is important to remember, that it is only the later flowering jackmanii type which is cut back now, not the early-flowering montana, which flowers in the early spring. If you have a cultivar of Nelly Moser, I would leave pruning of this until it has blossomed as this flowers on the old wood. So, the golden rule is, those that flower early, prune after flowering while those that flower late, prune now. Fuchsias need pruning back, towards the end of the month when it is time to give extra heat to get cuttings. It is worth considering partitioning off a small part of the greenhouse which you will be able to heat to a higher temperature. As you handle the plants, examine the labels and replace any which are becoming faint and unreadable.

CHOCOLATE PEPPERMINT SLICE

Ingredients

2oz soft brown sugar
4oz margarine
1 teaspoon cocoa
4oz S.R. flour
1 pinch salt
4oz icing sugar
Peppermint essence
4oz chocolate

Cream sugar and margarine until soft and creamy; stir in dry ingredients. Spread the mixture on to a greased flat tin (swiss roll tin) and bake in a moderate oven Mark 5 or 375°F for 20 minutes.

While still hot, mark into fingers and leave to cool. Mix the sieved icing sugar with quarter of a teaspoon peppermint essence and a little water. Spread over the biscuit mixture and leave to set. Spread with melted chocolate and when cold, cut into fingers.

March

SUNDAY MARCH 1 — March started with a wet day; it was absolutely bucketing down. I had a rotten cold and head and didn't get up until 9.00 am; this is very late for me. I sat by the fire most of the day, caught up with some of my mail and finished off my article for the *Deben Journal*. Later I sorted out slides for a film show which I am doing in the village to raise money for our Over 60's Christmas lunch. Friends called on me during the evening and we had an enjoyable time.

Monday March 2 — I felt much better today. Mr. Spicer gave me a rabbit which I soon skinned and put into salt water. Later I went to look after Russell and Sarah at Melton. At night, I went to the Parish Council meeting, nothing very exciting happened. So cold, the winds are at gale force today. I just hope my long fence doesn't fall.

Tuesday March 3 — Very sharp frost last night and the roads were rather icy when I went to Ipswich to record my gardening programme. Later, I looked in at the Ipswich Photographic Society's annual exhibition and found my portrait had won a cup for Mr. Bill Nash. He had taken the photograph in readiness for my trip to the U.S.A. I also went to Woodbridge to give blood; then after tea, I went to the village hall at Charsfield where I showed a selection of my slides of the village, which included several shots of local children at various social events over the years. These were enthusiastically received; it is always fascinating to note the changes which take place in the appearance of people and places over a period of time as revealed in old — and not so old — photos!

Wednesday March 4 — I went to Wivenhoe near Colchester to see my dear friend Seley Little, who has been checking over my manuscript. He took me out to lunch at a little restaurant in Wivenhoe. It was a pity the weather was so rotten, snowing on and off all day. Having left Seley's at 2.00 pm, I drove to Hadleigh where I gave an illustrated talk to the W.I. on gardening. Altogether, it has been a very busy day but most enjoyable.

Thursday March 5 — Went to the W.I. market; saw my first write-up in the *Deben Journal*. The editor told me that he had received some nice comments so this looks promising. I managed to get some trays of compost ready for pricking out some seedlings. In the afternoon, went to Earl Soham Over 60's club to show slides of the garden then after tea, went to Great Blakenham W.I. once more I showed slides of the garden. Another rather tiring day.

Friday March 6 — East winds blowing, rather cold on my back door. I had a few hours in the greenhouse pricking out seedlings and planting more seeds. Then off once more to do my gardening programme. On the way home, I called on friends Iris and Claude at Wickham Market. Iris has helped me with the final presentation of my manuscript which has to be off to the publishers this week.

As I drove along, I heard on my radio in the car that a British ferry boat "Herald of Free Enterprise" had tipped over and was sinking off Belgium with possibly six hundred passengers on board.

Saturday March 7 — I woke up early and put on my radio to hear the latest news of the ferry. My God! it's terrible — still two hundred people missing and a lot of children are known to be on board. The winds are still very cold. I got on with my mail, then pricked out more seedlings. After lunch, I went up to the Village Hall car park to meet two members of the Parish Council, Mrs. Joan Laurie and Richard Kitson. We planted forty shrub roses which Mr. Douglas Goldsmith of Ufford had kindly given us.

Hopes were fading of finding more people alive on the ferry. It is the worst accident, in peacetime at sea. Apparently the boat capsized so quickly that there was no time to send out an S.O.S. The tragic thing was that she was in Zeebrugge harbour, just two miles from shore. A very sad business.

After tea, I went to Hintlesham to show my garden slides; this was in aid of the appeal fund for Macmillan Nurses.

Sunday March 8 — Still very cold with the wind remaining in the east. Went in to my greenhouse and did some more tidying up, moving some pots around to make room for seed trays. Despite the wind, it is surprising how warm it gets in the greenhouse these days if the sun comes out. I still can't get over the bad news of the ferry which turned over on Friday evening; seeing the pictures on the TV and watching the families as they went over to identify their loved ones, was very harrowing. At the moment, the numbers of people dead is fifty-three, with eighty-two still missing, thankfully four hundred and eight persons are alive. There is talk that the bow doors were not closed as the boat left the harbour. It is all very terrible.

Monday March 9 — I was about early this morning as I left for London at 6.45 am to go to the Ideal Homes Exhibition. I went with John Rowe from Radio Orwell; we saw Princess Margaret at the show. I was a little disappointed as I expected to see more garden lay-outs there but of course, it is essentially a show for home-makers. Travelled back with John to his home in Stowmarket where we edited the tapes we had made during the day and I got home at 9.30 at night, feeling very tired.

Tuesday March 10 — Very sharp frost this morning. I went and recorded my radio programme then called and had lunch with David and his wife, Norine. My next trip was to Layer-de-la-Haye, near Maldon in Essex where I gave a talk to over one hundred Senior Citizens, on gardening; got home at a quarter to five. After tea I went down to Wickham Market to do some more checking on the manuscript and we worked until half-past ten — once again I didn't need any rocking to sleep!

Wednesday March 11 — A lovely sunny morning — such a change — but there was a frost early. Did some catching up with the mail, tidied up the house, did some washing, sorted out more seeds to plant in the greenhouse. Sent for my visa to visit the U.S.A.

After lunch I went to Old Newton Over 60's club, to show slides, then after tea, went back to Iris's for more checking on my manuscript.

Thursday March 12 — This has been an awful week for frosts, several of them very sharp. I went to Woodbridge to take my article for the paper. David and Norine came over and we went to Easton White Horse for lunch. The sun was really warm today. (I collected five eggs from my six hens today). This evening I have been to Rushmere to give my talk on "Akenfiield" I noticed the little cottage near the Chapel is up for sale, over £45,000 — what a price!

Friday March 13 — Spent the morning doing housework, cleaning brass, etc. As the winds were so cold, I brought compost and pots indoors and planted more seeds then popped them into the propagator. I did the Gardening Hour programme, then went right on to Hintlesham Gardening Club, to do a lecture about the Show bench. Got home at 11.00 pm feeling rather tired and very cold.

Saturday March 14 — Had such a rough night, my legs were aching and I had cramp so bad, it must have been due to standing in Hintlesham Village Hall the previous evening. Ronnie pulled my garden down, and we planted four rows of onion sets, two rows of spinach and five rows of parsnips. It is still very cold and even the frost still stays in the land, especially where the fence shades the garden — the sun doesn't get down to the soil there. It is unbelievable to think that, in the middle of March, the land is still so cold. I think the seasons must be changing. I had an early night for a change, as I was in bed by 10.00 pm.

Sunday March 15 — Woke up feeling much better. I did my articles for the local paper then went into the large greenhouse and did more work, moving plants around; also started to give a little extra water and a little feed. It is surprising now how the plants have dried out. The sun is getting more power although the nights are still cold. In the evening, I went back to Iris's and we finished checking my manuscript for the book.

Monday March 16 — Snow showers this morning; pity the poor birds — it always happens as they start to build their nests. I potted up a lot of my begonias, some of the corms are quite large so I split them into three.

   Packed my manuscript up and sent it to the publishers, I hope they will like it.

Tuesday March 17 — Had to take my car into Woodbridge to have a new exhaust fitted, they don't seem to last long these days. Also had my hair set. Tonight, I took part in a gardening quiz at the Woodbridge Ladies' Club; the other guests were Arthur Borrett, Roy Lacey and Beth Chatto. Mr. Charles Notcutt was the question master. The club is trying to raise money for the Macmillan Nurses and Cancer Fund. We had a most enjoyable evening and £600 was raised for the funds. When I came out, my car was all iced up so it doesn't look as if we are out of winter yet.

Wednesday March 18 — I went and did my "Peggy's Patch" on

Radio Orwell. The village was white this morning with snow and as I drove down the Debach road, I saw that the rooks had started to build their nests. It is strange how the pattern of life goes on with the birds nesting although there is still snow on the ground. I spent the evening writing letters to friends.

Thursday March 19 — Went to the W.I. market in Woodbridge, then had lunch with Jackie and the grandchildren; came home and did more work in the greenhouses. The seedlings have to be watched now as the sun can soon scorch them and you can even lose them. In the evening I went to Dales Road, Ipswich to give a talk and show slides of the garden to a Parent/Teachers Association, a lot of people were there and the talk seemed to go down very well.

Friday March 20 — I was about early this morning; did my gardening notes and sorted out the mail, then I got the spare bedroom ready for re-decoratng. A friend, George Woods, came as he is going to do the paintwork for me. After shifting the furniture around I planted more seeds and even brought some compost indoors to warm up ready for planting tomorrow. I believe in warming up the compost before sowing seeds as it takes a long time to do so, if left out when the air is so cold.

Saturday March 21 — Rather a dull start to the day but the clouds soon cleared and it became a lovely Spring day. I cleaned my car then filled the greenhouse tanks up with water and also planted a lot of seeds. The main greenhouse is becoming packed out but as we are having cold nights I don't like to move the pots into a cool greenhouse just yet. It has been one of the coldest March months for a long time.

Sunday March 22 — Another bonus today with the bright sunny weather. I went to Hoo Church at 8.30 for the early service, it is so peaceful at Hoo. This morning, many of us had the families who were lost in the ferry accident, on our minds. The boat is still lying on its side, with so many people still missing. Talking of missing, there is still no news about Terry Waite.

Allan, Jackie and the children came to tea and we had a lovely time. The children collected the eggs from the chicken's nest boxes — this is a job they love doing.

Monday March 23 — I started to have my house re-wired for electricity today. The winds are still very cold but as I took Sally for a walk up the lane, I noticed the primroses are coming out although on short stalks as yet. Tonight I went to the W.I. Group meeting at Great Cressingham near Swaffham in Norfolk, just 60 miles away, to give my "Akenfield" talk. My friend, Sheila, came with me for company; it is rather nice to have someone with you when travelling in the dark. We had a good journey and were back home by 10.45.

Tuesday March 24 — I went and recorded my radio programme today then went and bought some concrete slabs for my garden paths as I find that where the visitors walk, we have a lot of bare patches. In the evening went to Tooleys Court, an Old People's Home in Ipswich, to give them a slide show. This makes a nice change for them and they do enjoy seeing the pictures.

Wednesday March 25 — This morning I managed to get my small bedroom straight, then I did some gardening notes and letters. In the afternoon, I went to talk to a church group at Burlington Women's Fellowship in Ipswich, then in the evening, went to Levington Horticultural Society to give a talk on Flower Shows and what the judges look for on the Show bench.

Thursday March 26 — Went to the W.I. market then had lunch with Jackie and the grandchildren. Allan borrowed my car to take items to the rubbish dump, I went with him and was amazed to see what people throw away. On coming home, I pricked out more seedlings. Tonight I went to the Great Bromley Cheshire Home to give a talk and got home at 10.45, feeling, I must confess, rather tired.

Friday March 27 — Spent the morning writing up my gardening notes etc. Gales were blowing around the coast today and several trees had come down. I felt rather worried about my wooden greenhouse as it began to creak at times. We had rain, hail and thunder, in fact it was an awful day. I went to Ipswich to do my programme but I was glad to get home again.

Saturday March 28 — What a day, raining all the time. I went to Lakenheath with Sheila to open Lakenheath Village Home. This Home is for persons over 65 years and who have, in the main, lived in the parish for a minimum of ten years. It has been donated to the village and is run by the Trustees of the Christian Enterprise Foundation, which is registered with the Charity Commissioners as a charitable trust, and although this is a Christian based home, it is completely inter-denominational and is not directly associated with any one particular church. I had a lovely day and was treated just like a queen. They had a neat wooden plaque in the hallway of the Home which I was asked to unveil. I found it very pleasant meeting the old people and enjoyed a marvellous spread which had been laid on. We left late in the afternoon and arrived home at about 6.30 pm. I then went babysitting for Allan and Jackie. We moved the clocks forward one hour tonight, so hopefully we shall get some decent Spring weather now.

Sunday March 29 — Nice bright day. I'm amazed how quickly the birds eat the peanuts which I have hung out in nets. A pound's worth lasts only two days and even the sparrows hang on to the nets and feast on the nuts. I found a robin's nest in my potting shed; it was rather lovely, how she had made it amongst some plastic bags which were packed away in an old compost bag. In the evening I went and had a meal with Allan, Jackie and the children.

Monday March 30 — I notice a mole has run though my parsnip-seed bed — it looks as if they are going to be a problem again this

year. Spent some time trying to make more room in my greenhouse (it is always a problem at this time of the year). The
contract for my second book came today. It made a nice change,
having tea in daylight for the first time this year and afterwards
I did some gardening notes in the evening.

Tuesday March 31 — Started to make up my hanging baskets
today; I find it pays to plant them up early and I keep mine in the
greenhouse until the end of May, mainly planted with fuchsias
and geraniums. Bedding plants can be added to the baskets later.
The last day of this month reminds me of the old saying, "The last
day went out like a lamb, so we shall see what April will bring".

March has been a disastrous month, so many terrible things
have happened. First we had the Zeebrugge disaster, then we had
100 mile-an-hour winds whipping across the country, leaving
nine people dead and power lines down across East Anglia. At
Great Cornard near Sudbury, a shopping centre roof blew off for
the second time in twelve months. We also heard that the
Ipswich Odeon was under threat of closure; twenty-seven thousand people signed a protest and now they want to turn it into a
five-screen cinema. Locally, we heard that the Phyllis Memorial
Home at Melton is to close, despite local opposition.

HINTS FOR MARCH

The soil should be warming up, so plant shallots, onion sets and broad beans. You could also sow a few early lettuce, radish and carrot seed. At this time of the year, it is a matter of what to leave undone rather than what to do, but make sure that all seedlings and young plants in the greenhouse are shaded from the strong sunlight. This will prevent shrivelling, scorch and rapid drying out, all of which will severely damage growth. Give spring cabbages a top dressing of sulphate of ammonia or nitrate of soda as this will boost growth.

The tips of geraniums and fuchsias root easily at this time of the year and flowering pot plants will need feeding every seven to fourteen days, until the end of October while amaryllis will need regular feeding in order to form next years flower heads — don't cut off the leaves.

When pruning roses, the Hybrid Tea will need to be pruned hard while the Floribunda (cluster) will need only medium attention. Thin out the old wood, at the same time removing dead, diseased, damaged and any crossing branches. This needs to be done with a pair of sharp secateurs, by making a cut one centimetre above a bud and sloping slightly away from the bud. After pruning, I like to spray with Jeyes Fluid (2 teaspoons to one gallon of water), not only the plants but also the ground around the roses as this will help to kill any 'black spot' spores.

Plant gladioli four to five inches deep, place the corms on dry sand as this helps them to root better and also ensures good drainage at the base.

With the hedgerows coming into leaf, it is a sure sign that the soil is warming up and preparations can be made for sowing a wide range of plants. However, take my advice and do not attempt to work the soil if it is still wet and sticky. We have an old saying that when the farmer walks into the middle of the field, pulls his trousers down and sits on the bare soil, he can feel if it is fit to sow corn, but I am not suggesting that you do this in your garden. Salad vegetables can be grown but do watch the seedlings as birds can be a great problem. My brother will put black cotton over the rows as soon as the seedlings appear. Birds don't like cotton as they can't bear to feel it on their wings. Another method of keeping the seedlings safe is by putting netting over the seed beds. Another job is to thin out the seedlings as soon as they can be singled without damaging adjacent plants — you will find that this helps them to mature more quickly.

Herbs can be propagated now and you can also sow seeds of basil, borage, chervil and others. I like to sow my parsley in pans in the greenhouse, then prick them out to plant in the garden. I also make up hanging baskets, using parsley and dwarf marigolds — never mind the old wives tale that if you transplant parsley, you will have bad luck.

Plant the early potatoes now. Try to place the tubers on some bulky organic material as this will help to prevent scab disease.

PASSION CAKE (Irresistible)

Ingredients
6oz dark brown sugar
2 large eggs
7 fluid oz oil (Corn or
                Sunflower)
5oz finely grated carrot
2oz mixed chopped nuts
Pinch of salt
$3/_4$ level teaspoon
        bircarbonate of soda
6oz plain flour
$1/_2$ level teaspoon cinammon
$1/_2$ level teaspoon mixed
                  spice

For Icing
6 oz sifted icing sugar
3oz cream cheese
1 teaspoon lemon juice
1oz chopped mixed nuts

For Filling
3 to 4 tablespoons strawberry
jam

1 x 7in to 8in moule à
manqué or cake tin (base
lined and oiled)

Set oven Gas Mark 3 or 325°F

With wooden spoon work sugar and egg together, stir in oil, carrot and nuts. Sift all other ingredients together, then stir into carrot mixture, mixing well. Turn into prepared tin and bake in the centre of oven for about <u>one hour</u>, or until firm and springy, or use two $6^{1}/_2$ in sandwich tins, base lined, and bake at same temperature for 25 to 30 minutes. Turn out on a wire rack to cool.

     In a bowl, cream the cheese until soft, beat in lemon juice and gradually mix in the icing sugar and half the nuts. When cake is cold, trim if necessary and split into two layers, then sandwich together with jam. Spread the icing all over the cake then sprinkle the rest of the nuts around the edge of cake.

April

WEDNESDAY APRIL 1 — What a day, pouring with rain most of the time. I went to Ipswich to do my programme and then carried on to do another gardening lecture at an Old People's Home in Ipswich. In spite of the rain, I noticed the hedges were starting to burst out and also the first signs of the daffodils coming into bloom. It is encouraging too, seeing all the green shoots coming up in the hedgerows.

Thursday April 2 — As I walked up the path to feed my chickens this morning, I was thrilled to find a blackbird's nest containing five eggs, in one of my holly shrubs. Never went to the W.I. market today but did manage to take one hundred fuchsia cuttings and in the evening I went to Kessingland near Lowestoft, to give my "Akenfield" talk to a large group of W.I. members. It is remarkable how many people show a keen interest in the Suffolk dialect. As I came home along the A12, I saw the lovely Church of the Holy Trinity at Blythburgh, all lit up with floodlighting. It is a moving sight to see this magnificent building on the edge of the marshland. Blythburgh is certainly one of my favourite churches in the area.

Friday April 3 — I pruned my roses, today; also planted a Prunus Cherry tree in our village car park. Our retiring chairman, Mr. R. Kitson, is leaving the village to live in Framlingham, he has been Parish Council Chairman for over twenty years; he gave me the tree to plant as a memento of his time here.

In the evening I went to Ipswich, did my programme, then drove on to Sudbury where I was the guest speaker at the Horticultural Society's dinner. It went well, but I found I was rather tired afterwards. It is a bit much, giving a talk the same evening as doing a radio programme.

Saturday April 4 — Rather a damp day. I stayed inside and did my gardening notes for the local paper, then did some housework. After lunch, I did some work in the greenhouses, to make more room. This gets more of a problem day by day. This evening I went to the village pantomime which was "Snow White and the Seven Dwarfs". It really was a good show and reminded me again, how much talent there is in village community activities these days.

Sunday April 5 — What a lovely day; the sun was up early and it made me feel good to be out. I spent nearly all day in the greenhouse, pricking out plants; asters, lobelias, mimulus, impatiens and zinnias. The temperature registered 110 degrees at times. My brother, Ronnie, took my old fibreglass pond lining out as it had been leaking. I am undecided whether to concrete the pond out or to buy a new lining. I also pricked out red brussels sprouts today, something new to try.

Monday April 6 — Another lovely day; it seems more like June than April. Went to look after little Sarah as Russell had to go to see an ear specialist. He is having trouble with his hearing. This visit gave me a chance to do Allan's pruning — then I came home and did the rest of my own pruning as well. Cleaned a lot of pots and got out a lot more seed trays. Gone are the days when we used to mix up all our own compost, I know it would be cheaper but, with the vast amounts of various compounds available, it is so easy to use them although perhaps a bit more pricey.

Tuesday April 7 — Pouring with rain all day. Went to Ipswich and recorded my programme, then on to Mickfield to see Mr.

Michael Burch, who is a pond and fish specialist. After some thought, I bought a new liner for the pond, this will save a lot of work and concrete would take a long while to dry out. When I got home I potted up some herbaceous plants which had been grown from seed last Autumn (even if it does rain, there are always jobs to do in the greenhouses). Tonight, it is the Annual General Meeting of our parish church, St. Peter's. It amazes me how so many churches keep going as the quota rises every year. How do they expect villages to raise some two thousand pounds each for the Diocese before the actual running costs of their own churches are taken into account?

The ferry boat "Herald of Free Enterprise" was raised today, after having capsized a month ago. Over one hundred bodies were taken from it; how dreadful and what an appalling job for the divers.

Wednesday April 8 — Some begonia seedlings arrived in the post this morning; I pricked them out early, then called on Aunt Lizzie and Uncle Morry at Saxmundham; Uncle is still very ill — I took them some eggs, home-made soup and the first bunch of primroses. I then went on to Walberswick to have lunch with the Reverend Cecil Fox and his wife, Addy; he used to be the vicar of our parish (five years ago). It was nice to have a chat about old times and to give them all the village news. I then gave a talk to the W.I. at Walberswick and this went down very well. When I got home I cooked tea and afterwards planted out the first lettuce plants. I also cut a lot of spinach, fifteen bags in all and packed these ready for the W.I. market at Woodbridge.

Thursday April 9 — Went to the W.I. market and called in to see the grandchildren on my way home. I then started to tidy up the herbaceous borders, moving some plants around but a violent thunderstorm sent me scurrying into the greenhouse, so I potted up some begonias from trays into pots. My conservatory is very colourful at the moment with camellias full of red blooms and pots of primroses and polyanthus of all colours.

Friday April 10 — I found another blackbird's nest containing two eggs, in the garage today and my robin's nest has five eggs. I did my gardening notes then went outside, pricking out seedlings in the greenhouse. I also found another bird's nest in the potting shed; they must be very busy at the moment.

Had a letter from friends, Joan and Bob Morrison from New Jersey, U.S.A. today, asking me to stay with them after I have done my gardening lectures in the States in October; I had met them a few years back, as they usually come to stay for a few months each year in Dallinghoo. Mr. Morrison has all his text books on chemistry printed in Bungay.

Saturday April 11 — Very cold today with gale-force winds around. I spent all the morning working in the greenhouse. A lady from the village brought me some frog's spawn, which I put in my pond, after I had cleared it of weeds. It is strange how many people now have a job to find frog's spawn and in some places, the frog has become extinct.

After lunch, I did my Easter baking as it was so miserable outside. For the last two nights I have been in bed by 9.45 as my legs have been so painful — this must be due to all the standing I do during the day.

Sunday April 12 — Went to Hoo Church at 8.30 for early service, then called in on an old friend, for coffee. It was a typical April showers day. Ronnie, my brother, finished tidying up my pond while I did a lot of writing, answering letters from listeners to my radio programmes, on various aspects of gardening etc. Sarah is two years old today, so I went and had tea with them all; how my late husband, Ernie, would have loved to see his grandchildren — it makes a lump come into my throat when I think of these things but it is no good living in the past, you have to keep thinking of tomorrow. My legs feel much better today.

Monday April 13 — I spent the morning clearing up the house, then I cooked high tea as Alan Lee, from Radio Orwell was coming to have a meal; he was going to give a talk to our local W.I. about being a disc jockey.

My youngest son, David, rang to say that he had been promoted to sergeant in the Police Force, but he will have to work from Stowmarket. Again, I can only say that Ernie would have been proud of him; he has worked hard.

Tuesday April 14 — I was hit by a bug today and was so sick in the early hours of the morning, but I managed to go and record my "Peggy's Patch" programme. I called in to see David, to congratulate him, and as the day wore on, I began to feel better. I didn't do much in the evening, just rested for a change and had an early night.

Wednesday April 15 — A glorious day. I went to Woodbridge early and took my article in for the local paper, then came home and moved my plants around in the greenhouse. I pricked out more seedlings and after lunch, went to Diss to give a talk to a group of retired people and showed the "Akenfield" slides. After I got home I cooked tea, then went outside and did some weeding; the birds were singing and it was just like a June evening. I noticed that the eggs were gone out of the blackbird's nest in the garage and wondered what had taken them — my brother says that a mouse will get in the nest, and even magpies; there are several of these around here at the moment.

Thursday April 16 — What a bonus, we still have fine weather! I went and helped at the W.I. market. Little Russell went into hospital today, to have some problems sorted out with his ears. I had a pleasant afternoon in the garden, weeding and potting up small plants, it is surprising how much you can get from small pieces of herbaceous material. Tonight, I went to Bentley to give a talk on my garden, at the Horticultural Society and I think the talk went down very well.

Friday April 17 — I just cannot believe the weather, it is so warm. My brother put my potatoes in and I went to help my friend, Perry Branton, to decorate Hoo Church for her son's wedding. It looks so pretty with the Spring flowers. Russell had his operation today and it has gone well. As there was no Gardening Hour on Radio Orwell I did a lot of weeding this evening. Today is the hottest Good Friday for forty years, or so it has been reported.

Saturday April 18 — Yet another beautiful morning. I picked Perry up and took her to Ipswich where we did the flowers at the Town Hall ready for her son's reception. I came home and planted carrots, beetroot and radish seeds, also planted out Golden Acre cabbage plants, red cabbage and cauliflowers. Had a very busy time in the garden then I went and did the flowers in Charsfield Church ready for Easter. My Mother's grave is a picture, with all the primroses growing there it is completely covered with blooms.

Sunday April 19 — Went to the early service at Hoo Church. Today, it is so oppressively hot, I just don't feel like doing much. Had some friends in for lunch. Spent the afternoon resting and enjoying each other's company. In the evening, took Sally for a walk up the lane where she enjoyed herself chasing a rabbit, she certainly does not seem to mind the heat although coming back she was content to walk beside me. Had an early night for a change.

Monday April 20 — Rather dull at first and still no rain. I had a morning helping Ronnie plant the dahlia tubers. I know it is rather early but I have taken a chance, I shall have to watch the weather. I also potted up two hundred fuchsia cuttings and they look very well. During the afternoon the weather changed — it tried to rain.

Tuesday April 21 — The morning is still overcast. I spent the early part of the day sorting out my mail and catching up with paperwork. Afterwards I took a lot more fuchsia cuttings. After lunch, I had my first coach party from Harris's at Grays in Essex. Although they call eight times a year as my garden is one of the featured attractions on their seasonal schedules, this was unexpected.

Wednesday April 22 — Went to Eddie Goulding's Fuchsia Nursery at Bentley, to get some new plants, then on to Ipswich to do my gardening programme. Called on Mike and Eileen Riches, some friends in Ipswich then collected some compost on the way home. After tea, I went to the Salvation Army in Ipswich to give a talk to their Ladies Group.

Thursday April 23 — Went to help at the W.I. market then called on Jackie and the children. Their garden is looking lovely now that all the spring flowers are coming out. I had some friends call and I gave them lots of seedlings; it was so warm we were able to sit outside and have a cup of tea on the lawn. Tonight, I went to Stutton Horticultural Society, near Ipswich, to give a slide show on Country Views of East Anglia — these include scenes of Constable Country and the Stour Valley together with pictures of Norwich and Ipswich. I also include in this show slides of some of the well-known villages and small towns with which we are blessed.

Friday April 24 — Another lovely day. I got outside early and moved seed trays and plants into the cold frame, also finished potting up a lot of border plants ready to sell to visitors later in the year. I felt that I had achieved quite a lot today. The birds were singing and it was heaven just to be working in the garden. After tea, I went to Ipswich to do my programme.

Saturday April 25 — Still warm weather is with us. I went to judge at the Martlesham Spring Show today; it was lovely to see all the spring flowers as well as the many petite arrangements. When I got home, I changed back into my old working clothes and took a lot more cuttings from various plants. Ronnie gave the grass a cut and a good feed; I saw my first swallow today. Another blackbird's nest is in the hedge at the top of the garden and my robin has hatched out, so at last I can get into the shed more easily. My friends Pat and Ruby Welton, came in the afternoon and after tea, I showed them slides of my earlier week-end visit with them.

Sunday April 26 — My friends didn't leave until one o'clock this morning so I had a bit of a lie-in. When I went out I first checked my neighbour's greenhouses and chickens as he is away for the week-end. I also went to the "Save the Children Fund" Craft Show at Woodbridge as I was invited as their guest to answer any questions on gardening. Ronnie has been very busy this week-end, putting holes in bottles which I will later fill with compost and plant cuttings. These I shall hang on the fence as they make unusual but attractive containers.

Monday April 27 — The expert weather people can hardly believe the weather which we are having — it is more suited to the middle of summer than late spring. I moved one half of my greenhouse shelving out so as to be able to plant my tomatoes in growbags. In the afternoon I baby-sat with Russell and Sarah and it was so hot that we just sat in the garden. This evening I went to the Parish Council meeting. The "Herald of Free Enterprise" which went over fifty-two days ago, was today pulled into Zeebrugge harbour. They are still looking for bodies.

Tuesday April 28 — Another nice day. I went outside early and planted nine tomato plants in the greenhouse, then moved other plants around taking some outside. I know this is a bit risky but it is a chance I will have to take. John Rowe, a friend of mine, came to put some new outside lights up for me.

Wednesday April 29 — It is still so very hot, it is difficult to know what to wear. After I did my radio programme I went to a large

W.I. Group at Thorpe-le-Soken in Essex where over two hundred ladies were present and the meeting went well. I had a job to get away as so many people wanted to chat after I had given my talk but I eventually arrived home at 10.30 pm. I then packed fifteen bags of spinach for the market.

Thursday April 30 — Was woken up at 2.00 am by a violent thunderstorm. It was pouring with rain but at least it will do the garden good. All of a sudden, everywhere has turned green, hedges and trees are all bursting out into leaf. My two spring clematis, Ruby and Blue Macropetala, are looking very pretty on the garden fence and as I was washing dishes today, I noticed a thrush had started to build in my honeysuckle, only five yards from the back door. The garden is looking delightful at the moment, with all the spring flowers in bloom.

I cannot remember April being so warm as it has been during these last two weeks; it is all very pleasant but the bulbs, especially the daffodils, cannot stand the heat and they have not lasted very long. The warm weather is really going against nature.

The *East Anglian Daily Times* reports that East Anglia has put the Riviera in the shade as Easter temperatures soared to 72°F.

The local radio news stated that in Harwich, people don't like the idea of a Sealink Car Ferry being used as a temporary detention centre for the Tamil refugees.

HINTS FOR APRIL

One job which I always enjoy in the garden, is to make hanging baskets and I like to find different varieties of plants to try out if possible. However, the first thing to do is to line the basket by standing it on an upturned bucket and securing the hook from a length of wire. Moss is ideal as a liner, if you can get it but if not, peat, foam or black polythene can be used, with a soil-less compost. First plant the centre bottom of the basket, by pushing small plants through the chains, then fill up the sides and finally plant the top. Some useful plants are trailing lobelia, busy lizzies, geraniums, fuchsias, marigolds, petunias, foliage plants helichrysum Nepeta and ferns. Also, do try pink diascia planted with basket-type verbena — it makes a very attractive basket.

Now is the time to thin out herbaceous plants, like delphiniums, lupins and phlox (they will respond to thinning out) to leave 5 or 6 shoots on the plants. Old clumps of herbaceous perennials will benefit from lifting and being divided — I try to do my borders every third year.

If you have a pond, remove any dead plants and this is a good time to plant water lilies — old overgrown plants may be taken out and divided. Check stakes and ties, especially after strong winds. Remove old brassica stumps, such as cabbage and brussels sprouts, but do use an old fork, as you can soon ruin the tines of a good one.

Transplant bulbs which have been forced, when the leaves die down. I make a small trench and line it with an old piece of wire netting, turned up at both ends. Place the bulbs on the netting and cover them with soil. When you want to find the bulbs later in the year, you then just lift at each end of the wire netting and you will be able to collect all the bulbs at once.

Sow French beans now, also marrows and sweet corn, where cloches are available. Sweet corn can be started off in pots in the greenhouse but do be careful when planting out, not to disturb the roots in order not to check the growth. Keep buckets of water in the greenhouse, also dampen the flowers as it helps to create good growing conditions.

Remember that April has spells of cold weather, such as the "blackthorn winter" and few areas escape night frosts except those very near to the coast. Such frosts will always be more severe over dry ground and again, frequent watering is good gardening practice.

Slugs and snails are busy attacking young crops, particularly lettuce and hostas, so save egg-shells when cooking, wash them and dry them in the oven when you have finished baking. Once they are hard, break them into small pieces and store in a tin ready for use. Place a few broken pieces round each plant — slugs and snails won't want to climb over the shells.

HONEYSUCKLE WINE

Ingredients

2 pints honeysuckle blossom
3lb sugar
$^1/_4$lb raisins or 4oz wine concentrate
1 lemon
1 orange
1 campden tablet
1 teaspoon grape tannin
1 gallon water
Yeast & nutrient

The flowers must be fully open and dry. Wash them in a colander, pour the water (cold) over them and stir in 2lb sugar, the minced raisins (or concentrate) and the citrus fruit juice. Add the crushed campden tablet. Stir well and next day, add the yeast (a Sauternes is suitable), tannin and nutrient. Ferment for a week in a warm place, stirring daily, then add the remaining sugar and stir well. Strain into fermenting jar, rack and bottle as usual. Use a half pound of sugar less for a really dry wine.

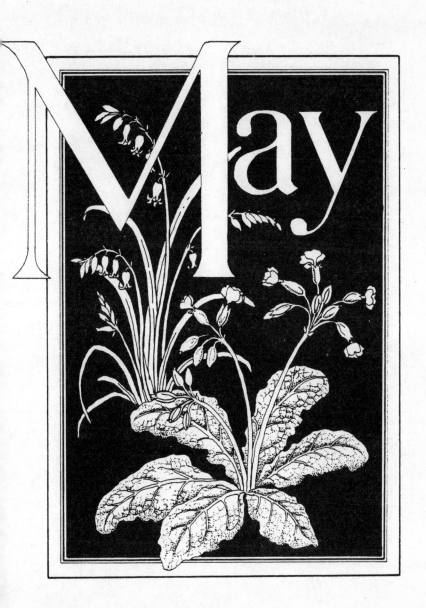

May

FRIDAY MAY 1 — Mayday today, but not as nice as last week, rather dull and wet. I spent the morning catching up with my correspondence. I get so much mail these days, with many people writing to the Radio Station with all sorts of queries, from gardening to folklore. I do wish that I could type or have a secretary. After tea, I went and did the gardening programme. We had a lot of people ringing in; we notice that this does vary from week to week, sometimes on the colder evenings, people are indoors and more ready to phone whereas, if it is warmer, they are in the garden and too busy to get in touch.

Saturday May 2 — I got up early today as I still had to write my weekly article for the local newspaper. The postman told me that there had been a very sharp frost and that he had to scrape the ice from the windscreen. I am glad I warned people last night not to put out their bedding plants. The weather got much clearer as the day wore on. I went up to the church and tended the graves of my husband and my parents. The churchyard looked so pretty with all the blossom on the cherry tree, together with all the wild flowers.

I planted up twelve half-baskets with busy-lizzies and small fuchsias, these of course will have to stay in the greenhouse for a time. I also cut eight lovely cauliflowers from the garden today, then I made one gallon of dandelion wine.

Sunday May 3 — I went to the early service at Hoo. It is still so very cold, with gale force winds. After church, I went on and had coffee with my second son, David. He took me to see a house he was thinking of buying, near Crown Point at Martlesham. The properties were selling for £66,000; a lot of money I thought, especially as there was not much garden. The houses in the scheme were detached, but there was only just room to walk in between each house. House prices have shot up so much in the past few weeks and I feel so sorry for the youngsters. You cannot buy a house for £25,000 any more and I feel that our young people in the villages will all be pushed out because of this. As this is an easy commuting area, executive types of people are tending to buy up any vacant properties.

Monday May 4 — Bank Holiday — Ronnie dug up the old cauliflower and sprout and broccoli land and also put in poles for the runner beans. I did a lot of weeding in the borders and planted flower seeds straight into the ground. It was not too bad a day and I feel quite satisfied as we have got through a lot of work. This evening, I racked some parsnip and dried fruit wine.

Tuesday May 5 — I had a lovely day as Allan, Jackie, and little Russell and Sarah came for the whole day. We had a good cooked lunch then went for a walk around the village. I am lucky as we can still see cows from my window and this is a sight you don't see very often today. The children wanted to go to see the baby calves in the field.

Another rather surprising thing happened today; a little robin started to build a nest in my wine shed, among the wine bottles. What a strange place to build. The baby robins from the top shed flew off today.

This evening I have been to Old Newton near Stowmarket, to give a talk to a W.I. group. A busy day and once again, I didn't need any rocking to sleep at bedtime.

Wednesday May 6 — Hooray! Today I went back to my old time on the radio — 11 am. It is much more convenient for me as I then have the rest of the day to do other things. I called to see friends in Ipswich, Jean and Peter Woods, who gave me a lot of fuchsia cuttings. I also called in to see my Aunt Vera, she is in hospital and has had a spinal operation. Visiting hospitals always makes me appreciate my own good health. In the evening I went to the Royal Hospital School at Holbrook to talk to the W.I. ladies.

Thursday May 7 — After going to the W.I. market, I came home and put my onion plants out (these were planted in boxes at Christmas time). I planted a lot of my dried flower seedlings out, including Helichrysum, Statice, Rodanthe and Acroclinium; this last one is especially pretty. Today we have had the County and Parish Elections. I was returned to serve another four years on Charsfield Parish Council — God willing. My daughter-in-law, Jackie, had hired a carpet cleaner for the day and she came over and cleaned my carpets, it was a kind thought; what it is to have a family!

Friday May 8 — Another nice day. I worked in the greenhouse moving plants around and putting trays of plants outside to harden off. I think people with greenhouses spend half their time at this season of the year, trying to balance and make space for various plants etc. After finishing my programme this evening on the radio, I went to the Town Hall in Ipswich and appeared on a Charity Quiz team for Hospital Radio, arriving home at 10.45, very tired indeed.

Saturday May 9 — Mrs. Hope-Thorpe, a lady from the village, was having a sale for Christian Aid Week, so I took her a lot of my plants to sell. It was so hot by lunchtime that it was nice to sit and rest for a while. I managed to put out a few pansies and stocks and although my fingers itched to put out more, I didn't think I would risk it. I got on with tidying and weeding the garden. Ronnie dug out one side of my greenhouse and after we took out the rest of the shelving, I planted the rest of my tomatoes straight into the ground. I am giving growbags a rest for a year or two; I know this means a lot of work and the soil will have to be removed each year, but we shall see.

When my brother left to go home at 11.30 pm, he called me to listen to the nightingale — this is a wonderful sound to hear late at night.

Sunday May 10 — I had two friends come to lunch today, Arthur Borrett who is a retired horticulturist, and Clifford Arbon who was a wheelwright. Cliff is in his 80th year (I think). My brother and I sat with these two very knowledgeable men, listening to their old-time reminiscences. We sat talking until 3.30 in the afternoon, it was a joy to hear them and we had a very pleasant time together.

In the evening I got together all my publicity ready to send off to the U.S.A. then I took Sally for a walk up the lane, where I picked enough young oak leaves to make up a gallon of wine.

Monday May 11 — Rather a dull morning. I went off early to the Post Office in Wickham Market, posting eight packages off to America, then continued on to Westleton where I gave a talk about my garden, to a group of ladies. I also called in at Mr. Fisk's Clematis Nursery in Westleton and bought five plants at £2 each. These were not very expensive as they were lost-label plants, however they are strong and were good value. I gave two of the plants to Jackie — it will be a surprise to see which variety they are when they come into flower. I also ordered two plants which will not be ready until the Autumn, Louise Rowe and Elsa Spath. On the way back, I stopped to take some photos of Westleton Church, it is very well-known for its Wild Flower Festivals in the summer months. The Church has a thatched roof, which is rather unusual.

I got back to Melton in time to baby-sit with Russell and Sarah and late in the afternoon I arrived back for tea. I noticed that there are now two eggs in the little robin's nest in my wine shed.

It is still rather gloomy so I think I will have an early night.

Tuesday May 12 — I had an early appointment at Saxmundham today, with a conservatory specialist. They are holding a two-day event in June and would like me to attend and advise on the kind of plants best suited for growing in conservatories. As I left Saxmundham, it hailed and thundered and really turned out to be a really terrible day. You always seem to get this sort of weather when the bedding plants are put out to harden off. Tonight I went to the Parochial Church Council meeting at the Vicarage, held to arrange the Annual Summer Fete and the Appeal Fund.

Wednesday May 13 — Went to Ipswich to do my programme — also took my venetian blinds in for repair. After lunch, I had a surprise when a visitor called, a Mr. Belfour, MBE, DHM, past President of the National Rose Society. He was on his way to Pontins to lecture to a gardening group and called in to see my garden. He would have liked to have stayed longer but he was pushed for time — it was an honour, to think that he had stopped to see my garden.

Thursday May 14 — It was pouring with rain when I got up, very heavy storms with hail stones again. I went to the W.I. market, took radishes and some pots of preserves, then went on to a Press meeting at the Suffolk Show Ground. The secretary, Mr. Hargreaves, outlined the programme for the coming show. I met up with old and new friends and very much enjoyed the meeting. Over lunch, which was quite a good lunch, we covered numerous topical issues. After I got home and had cooked tea, I went to the Battisford Ladies Group to give a talk. One thing I have noticed this week, is that the evenings are very cold. No wonder my little robin built her nest in a warm place; she has now laid five eggs.

Friday May 15 — Another stormy day. I went to the chiropodist early, then came home and, because the radio forecast a sharp frost tonight, I moved all the bedding plants into the garage.

Later, I sorted out slides as the Rev. and Mrs. Laurie are having a cheese and wine party in aid of the church and would like me to show slides of various events depicting old and new scenes of Charsfield. I did my radio programme and once more, didn't get home until a quarter to eleven.

Saturday May 16 — Up early again — at six o'clock and went to see if the frost had done any damage, but thankfully no sign of this. The local Village Flower Show Committee had a coffee morning and I took them some bits and pieces. From there I went and cleaned and scrubbed the gravestones on my husband's and parents' graves. The churchyard is still looking so pretty, with its wild flowers and I can quite understand why so many people don't like churchyards mown until the grass looks like a lawn.

I potted up a lot of fuchsia cuttings, also some half-hardy annuals. Ronnie cut the grass and did a lot of hoeing. I have tried a new scheme with my borders this year and I have planted parsley and pansies together. Mixing flowers and herbs and even vegetables, together, is a frequent talking point among gardeners just now, set off I believe, by one of the gardening programmes on TV. I also planted out two rows of red brussels sprouts and some sprouting broccoli. The weather has been quite warm at times today.

Sunday May 17 — Started to bed out some of my hardier bedding plants this morning, also tidied up the backyard garden but by lunchtime we had grey skies again and soon it was raining hard. The oldest resident in the village died today; he was Mr. H. Buckles, who had reached the grand old age of ninety-four. It is also the seventh anniversary since my dear husband, Ernie, died — what a lot has happened in the last seven years.

Monday May 18 — I was up really early this morning, at five o'clock, as I had to catch the 6.25 train from Ipswich to London to be at the Chelsea Flower Showground by nine o'clock. It was a wonderful sight, just standing and looking at the blooms. John

Rowe from Radio Orwell, was with me with his tape-recorder and I interviewed various people, among them was the Duchess of Devonshire and the Choirboy of the Year (they were promoting the naming of the rose "Christingle"); others I spoke to were Penelope Keith, Stephanie Lawrence, Susan Hampshire, Judith Chalmers, Julia Clements, Arthur Billett, Beth Chatto and Alan Titchmarsh. No matter how many times I go to the Show, I always enjoy this day. It is so wonderful meeting old friends and seeing all the new varieties of flowers which are brought out. After a mad rush round most of the Show, I arrived back home at half-past five, giving me just enough time to freshen up for the Parish Council meeting. It was the first time in twenty years that a lady was voted to take the chair — Mrs. S. Green. I was very thankful to get into my bed tonight.

Tuesday May 19 — It is amazing how, after a good night's sleep, you are ready to start once more. I was quite taken aback this morning, to read in our local paper, the *East Anglian Daily Times*, that a small local paper for which I had been writing, had gone bust; what a pity! I did some letters, then went to work in the greenhouse for a while.

After lunch, John came over with the tape which we made yesterday. We had got so much good material that it was quite a job to know what to cut out. By late afternoon, I was beginning to feel tired so, for a change, I stayed in for the evening.

Wednesday May 20 — I went to Radio Orwell and they played half the tape on "Peggy's Patch" — I think it went down well. I then went to Capel St. Mary to see Mr. and Mrs. Geary — he has done quite a few drawings for my book and also a very good sketch of Charsfield Church; he really is a very clever man with a pencil. I came home and moved more plants into the garage; the wind was blowing and it is still quite cold for May. I also got a punctured tyre on my car, but thank goodness, it happened when I was at home.

Thursday May 21 — Went to the W.I. market. It is so cold and wet and I cannot remember the month of May ever being so miserable, with all the north winds. The poor old bedding plants just cannot stand this weather and the little robin is sitting tight in the shed. I have to go in there very carefully when I want something out of the freezer.

My brother pulls my leg and tells me "You know why the robin built in the shed, she knew this cold weather was coming".

The grandchildren have made me a scarecrow — with their Mummy's help; it is supposed to represent a little boy and has to stand in the middle of my brassica plants.

Friday May 22 — Heavy storms today and very cold. My friends, Iris and Claude, came over and we drove to Norwich where I was the guest on the "Keith Skipper Programme" on BBC Radio Norfolk. We had quite a chat about "Akenfield" and my garden and also talked of the old country ways and of all the changes which we are experiencing now. They made me very welcome and I enjoyed myself. We got home about five o'clock and after a quick cup of tea, I went back to Ipswich where I did my radio programme.

Saturday May 23 — Yet another dull start to the day, with rain, but this cleared up by 11 am. Since then, I have had a good day finishing putting out bedding plants in odd corners around the garden and also filling up some containers. The garden is beginning to look very pretty and the lawns are a real picture. This is thanks to my brother; he does take pride in the grass. The garden opened for the season today, and we have had several visitors.

Sunday May 24 — Today started rather warm but it is still cold, I fear, for May. I went to Hoo Church at 8.30 am then got back home as the visitors started to arrive from ten o'clock onwards; it turned out to be a busy day as we had over one hundred and fifty people through the garden. Ron called me out at lunchtime to see a swarm of bees flying over the house — "A swarm of bees in May is worth a load of hay", so this surely must be a good sign. This evening it turned very cold so I lit a little fire, always a welcome treat when it is needed out-of-season.

Monday May 25 — Spring Bank Holiday — rather a dull start but by the middle of the morning it had turned out nice and warm. I was up early and planted some dahlias and also finished planting up some more containers. We had one hundred visitors through the garden; it is good to see old friends back again, to see our displays. Ron started his routine with the watering and feeding; it is one thing having containers, but it is another thing when you have to go round doing all the watering!

Tuesday May 26 — This morning I did some more planting of containers and tubs then put out two rows of sprouting broccoli. The first coach load of visitors came today, these were mainly from an over 60's Club. The ladies from the church provided cream teas at £1.50 per head; this not only enables the church to make some money but also adds considerably to the visitor's enjoyment of their outing.

As it began to get dark, I stood listening to the singing of a nightingale, it really is a wonderful sound in the quiet of the evening although their song will probably finish once their young leave the nest.

Wednesday May 27 — Up early today as it is Suffolk Show time. I took Ronnie and my friends, Iris and Claude, with me. Because this is the day on which I do my radio programme "Peggy's Patch", I was able to do all this from the Flower Show tent. The weather turned out very warm and we all had a lovely day looking at the various stands and meeting many friends. We particularly liked the working horses and one wonders whether we shall ever see them back on the farms — somehow I have my doubts. We decided to leave the Showground at about five o'clock, before the main rush got under way and we all came back home and had tea together. I think we were all glad to just kick off our shoes and sit down to rest for an hour or two.

Thursday May 28 — Went to the W.I. market then called in on Allan and Jackie and the children to tell them about the Show. I felt so tired today, I think it must be due to all the walking which I did yesterday at the Showground and trying to find ideas for future articles. As I walked round the garden in the evening, I saw that a rabbit had been eating some of my plants; I suppose there is no wonder, as I have seen so many in my neighbour's orchard and I think they come underneath the fence. I just hope that they don't do too much damage.

Friday May 29 — The first thing I did this morning was to get my letters and other correspondence out and tried to sort through them, this is not one of my favourite jobs, I have to admit, but which has to be done. I also had the coach from Harris's of Grays, call again today, bringing visitors from all parts of London. When they had left, I went and bought more potting compost as some of my fuchsias are in need of a little more, then went on and did my gardening programme.

Saturday May 30 — A really warm day, for a change. I did a lot of work in my greenhouse and also put some hanging baskets and bottles out (these are the bottles which have had small holes knocked in the bottom, and geraniums planted in them).

As it was my neighbour's turn to put flowers in the church, I did a large flower arrangement for her. At this time of the year, the garden always looks particularly lovely in the evenings; the first summer flowers are so fresh and dainty. Tonight, we went out for a celebration meal at Earl Soham — this week it was Ron's birthday as well as my friend, Iris's. When we came home, it was pouring with rain so this will do the garden a lot of good.

Sunday May 31 — My little robin has hatched her eggs and I stood at my kitchen window and watched the mother bird flying backwards and forwards into the wine shed with titbits for her young. As I watched, the blue-tits were busy as well, feeding their young brood. Nature is a wonderful thing.

Today turned out nice and warm and we had several people looking round the garden. I must admit that it begins to look very pretty but I don't know what I should do without all the help Ronnie gives me. The only bugbear is that we don't really have enough parking space for the visitors' cars.

Another eventful month has passed and has brought changes in the district which will certainly have an effect on many lives.

The millionaire publisher, Robert Maxwell, has taken over the engineering firm of Ransomes and Rapier at Ipswich, and this has brought a feeling of uncertainty and a lot of workers now feel that perhaps the old firm has had its day.

Also this month has seen the farewell of Bobby Ferguson from the Ipswich Town Football Club, after failing to win promotion in the play-offs. However, as one goes, another one comes and John Duncan from the Chesterfield club has taken over the reins at Portman Road.

HINTS FOR MAY

"First of May, first of May, Hedgerow loving starts today"

The garden is now coming into its glory, with all the lovely shades of green. There are so many jobs to do that it is difficult to know where to start. The main one is to keep the hoe going, to stop the weeds before they grow into plants. Greenhouses must be shaded, as the temperature gets very hot under glass. Prune early spring-flowering shrubs after they have flowered, such as forsythia and flowering currant and gradually harden off plants in the cold frames.

Dead-head shrubs and their flowering plants, remembering that most decorative plants flower better the following year when old flowers are removed as they fade. This process is best carried out before seed pods begin to form. I know that it is a tedious job, with plants producing many flowers, but it is worth it in the end.

Runner beans like well-prepared soil — my brother digs a trench in early November each year which we fill with all manner of rubbish. Come May, it is topped up with soil and the runner beans planted. This should grow beans as long as your arm! I like to keep my runner bean seed from year to year, and the following list can also be kept:- beans of all kinds, parsley, spinach, swedes and turnips, these are all good for a second season. Beet, carrots, leeks, lettuce, onions and tomatoes will last for three years while cabbage and kohl rabi will keep for up to six years. However, all these are well beaten by celery, celeriac, cucumbers, marrows and pumpkins, which keep for nine years. The one real exception is parsnips, these have a short life and it is not advisable to keep these for another year.

This is the time of year for dividing and re-planting Christmas roses and polyanthus. Keep an eye on tubs, troughs and other containers so that the soil does not dry out and give all the plants a liquid feed from now onwards, once a week. Take cuttings of herbs and alpines. Pinch out the tops of broad beans to discourage blackfly but don't throw them away as they make a tasty vegetable if boiled for a minute or two and served with cheese sauce.

It is now that I begin to put my hanging baskets outside also the two drainpipes which stand each side of my front door. These are $4^1/_2$ inches wide with holes cut in them diagonally. I then plant fuchsias in each hole and, by the end of the summer, you cannot see the pipes at all — the fuchsias just hang down and cover every inch.

ROSE PETAL JELLY

Ingredients

Dried rose petals
Apples
Preserving sugar

Make apple jelly with good cooking apples but do not peel them. Cut them up fairly small, put them in a preserving pan and cover with cold water. Simmer slowly to a pulp. Strain the pulp through a jelly bag and leave to drip all night. Measure the liquid and to every pint allow a pound of preserving sugar. Stir until the sugar is dissolved and then put in as many dried rose petals as the liquor will hold. Boil until the jelly sets, when tested on a cold plate. Strain before potting.

June

MONDAY JUNE 1 — I found one of my chickens sitting on a nest of eggs under the chicken hut today; she had gone broody but unfortunately, it was pointless as I have no cockerel. I went to a local farmer who let me have a sitting of eggs but he was not sure when they were due to hatch out. He was pretty sure that they had already been sat on for two weeks which meant that they had another week to go.

The garden is coming into its full summer glory now; the honeysuckle scent is wonderful at night while the lupins, pyrethrums and roses are all bursting into bloom. I saw a small rabbit in the garden again today.

Tuesday June 2 — What a surprise I had when I went to feed the chickens; two of the eggs from the sitting I had put under the broody hen yesterday, had already hatched. The poor old hen seemed a bit shocked but she looked very proud of her two little chicks.

It has been pouring with rain but this will help the bedding plants enormously. I went to Ipswich to a W.I. Home Economics meeting as I am on the committee. In the evening I went back to Ipswich, to a Suffolk Horticulture and Produce Association Committee meeting and later called on my friends, Jean and Peter Woods, in Ipswich and collected three more bags of compost from the nursery. When I arrived home, I found that Ron had made me a chicken coop while I had been away, he had used my Father's old army box.

Wednedsay June 3 — I went to Ipswich and took two hanging baskets to a friend, which I had made up for him. While there, I bought two tubs ready for planting up with begonias, a present for Jackie's birthday. When I got home I mixed up some sand and peat, ready to use for cuttings. I bought 14lb of sharp sand, for £1.28 and I thought to myself, fancy living in the country and having to buy sand! This afternoon, I called to see Sidney Moss, an old gardening friend — he is very knowledgeable and has spent a lifetime working as a gardener. Later in the day we had some heavy storms, but before this, as I came home, I stopped the car and picked a dozen ox-eye daisies (chrysanthemum leucanthemum), I love these flowers and used to pick bunches of them when I was a school-child. Unfortunately, you don't see many of them today although they are sometimes found in churchyards.

Thursday June 4 — I went to the W.I. market and then called on Jackie and the children; I took her two hanging baskets and the two planted tubs, for her birthday. Their garden looks very pretty and they have both worked very hard to get it round; Ernie would have been very pleased to see what they have done. I managed to get ten more chicks today from a farmer at Debach, to put with the other two. Ronnie made a corner of the chicken run into an enclosed area, so that the other hens would not harm them. Another worry in this respect is the magpies; they really are a problem these days, killing birds and stealing eggs. I had a 'phone call from Mr. Dick Freeman of Bredfield, to say that he had a spare cockerel, if I would like it. I went there at about 8.00 pm and he took me and showed me over the farm and to look at his cattle. The farm is just like a picture book, nothing in its place but he knows where to find things and his stock looks very healthy. He is the kind of farmer who loves his animals and is very kind to them. It took the best part of an hour, one which gave me great pleasure, looking around. Mr. Freeman still has many hedges and it really is like visiting a Suffolk farm of fifty years ago, to look round this lovely old place.

Friday June 5 — Sadly, my old hen has rejected the little chicks, I found one dead so I brought the others indoors and put them in a box with a hot water bottle and some food; they seem to be alright. Allan and Jackie brought the children to see the chicks and it was a treat to see how their faces lit up, when they caught sight of them.

Saturday June 6 — The winds are awful today, blowing the flowers and vegetables all over the place. Because of the wind, I took some of the hanging baskets down, just to be on the safe side and Ronnie tied up the beans and dahlias. The little chicks still seem to be doing well, I have put them in the cool greenhouse out of Sally's way as she is so jealous, and I think would very quickly dispose of them.

In the afternoon, I went to open a church fete at Winston, near Debenham. They met me with a pony and trap and I drove to the little field near the church, where the fete was being held and performed the ceremony from the trap. Shortly afterwards, there was an almighty thunderstorm and the heavens really opened — every one ran to the little marquee for shelter but fortunately, it only lasted for about half an hour. Today would have been our thirty-fourth Wedding Anniversary.

Sunday June 7 — Not a very bright day, raining on and off. I went to the 8.30 Holy Communion Service at St. Peter's, our village church in Charsfield, then came home and began sorting out some papers for my trip to the U.S.A.

The problems with my broody hen seem to have leaked out, as a friend in the village brought me a broody bantam — I tried my chicks under her and she seems alright, so I hope she will take to them. This evening has turned out cold so I had a little fire. Some friends came round to see my Chelsea slides.

Sally was knocked over today, by two boys riding down the lane on a motorcycle, I suppose she just got in their way. Poor little thing, she was so frightened but thankfully she was only grazed under the chin and on her paw.

Monday June 8 — It was pouring with rain when I got up, but the one bright spot is that the baby chicks seem to have taken to their new mum. I tidied the house, then went to Melton, babysitting. I took Russell and Sarah to feed the ducks at Wilford Bridge at Melton. This is a lovely area to take children as well as being a good picnic place. I was amazed how the children were picking out items of interest and asking me questions — what were the holes in the ground (the rabbit holes) and why were there mole hills all over the area? Still, I would rather have them asking questions, than going along without noticing anything, for this is one of the best ways to learn. We walked along the river wall and Grandma, in her wisdom, took a short cut or so she thought! We landed up in a boat yard and had to find our way back. The children thought I was rather silly to lose my way.

Tuesday June 9 — Another wet day! When will we get some warm, growing weather? Everywhere is muddy and all the trees are dripping wet; the baby chicks still seem to be alright but the chicken run is just like a mud-bath and how the chickens walk about through it all, is amazing. This afternoon, a coach-load of ladies came to see the garden and it did just manage to keep fine for them while they were here. I am afraid that I am an impatient person and I get very frustrated when I know that there is so much to be done in the garden, yet I am not able to do it.

Wednesday June 10 — A better day; I woke up to find the sun was shining. I went to do my programme in Ipswich but came home early as I had a coach-load of visitors coming from somewhere near Bury St. Edmunds. This evening, I have been to Stowmarket, as I took part in a quiz for a Gardening Question Time, which was being run by the Stowmarket Ladies Club. The promise of good weather did not last and on the way home it rained so hard that it was a terrible job to see to drive, and I didn't arrive home until half-past eleven.

Thursday June 11 — Bless me! — I woke up to hear it still raining. I didn't go to the W.I. market as Joan Morrison came in for coffee, then took me to the local pub for lunch. We had a good chat about my forthcoming visit to America where hopefully, I shall be staying with her in New Jersey, which is not far from New York. The rain did ease later in the day and I went to pick up a pig—a dead one!! —half for Jackie and half for me, to put in the freezer; I bought it from a local farmer, costing 67p per pound, which is very reasonable. We always know we will get good meat from this source.

I also had sixteen ladies from Battisford who called in to see the garden.

Friday June 12 — Went off early to Saxmundham today, with my car full of plants as I was giving hints to a newly-established conservatory designer and manufacturer, on what to grow in the conservatory. We had awful thunderstorms while I was there and at one time, hail fell as well! Afterwards, I looked in on my Uncle Morry; he is still very ill and looks a poor old thing.

Walking round the garden in the afternoon I noticed that the baskets are beginning to look very colourful — Ron does a good job looking after them so well. I also noticed my Nelly Moser clematis, it is a picture at the moment. Many of the shrubs in the garden are coming into all their glory. I think I must have got every little spot filled up, even the vegable garden is full just now. I am cutting spring cabbage and spinach. My little robins flew out of the wine shed today; I do hope they weren't tipsy!!

Later on, I picked up my old friend, Arthur Borrett, as he was a guest for the evening on the radio programme. I had a look at his garden, which is very pretty, and he has some interesting foliage plants, in particular.

Saturday June 13 — I started the day early, having to remove some of the hanging baskets from the coal-shed door as I had some of my winter fuel delivered; one ton of Anthracite Stovesse nuts — £163, what a price!

It was rather a nice morning, a pleasure to be outside. I tidied up the rest of my seed trays and also my top garden sheds.

At 1.30 pm, I went back to Saxmundham to give further advice on plants, to the new Conservatory firm. After a busy afternoon, I arrived home at five o'clock to find several people waiting to ask me questions. After tea, I finished planting in some more tubs, but this had to be done in between the frequent storms.

Sunday June 14 — More heavy rain, which kept me awake during the night. I think that a part of the water guttering is blocked as I could hear the water over-flowing. We had an early lunch today, after which I went back to Saxmundham. It is surprising how many people came along, despite the cold, to see about having an extra room added to their homes. Having a conservatory built seems to be the "in thing" today.

Reaching home, one of the first jobs I did was to light a fire and I thought, fancy needing a fire in June!! In the early evening, some friends from Radio Orwell came round to discuss their wedding flowers, which they have asked me to do for them, in August. Later, Claude and Iris came over and it was nice just to sit by the fire and have a glass of wine to warm us up. On a cold evening, I can think of nothing nicer than enjoying the company of good friends around a warming drink.

Monday June 15 — A quiet day. After I had done some jobs in the house and some weeding in the garden, I went to see Jackie, my daughter-in-law, as it is her birthday today, and I gave her a Flowering Cherry tree to go with the hanging baskets and tubs which I had already taken. Allan had the day off, so later, they brought the children over to see the baby chicks again. We also walked over the road to see the cows with their baby calves, and the peacocks. The children were so pleased to see the animals and it is so good that they can see them when they are really alive and not just as pictures in books; in fact, it is remarkable how many people do stop to see the cattle in the field.

Tonight I have been to Woodbridge Library for a talk — this

was for the Historic Society and it was rather strange that I met an American lady who now lives in my old school at Kettleburgh. We had a "rare" chat and she invited me to go down to see what they had done to the old place. There still seems to be a lot of bad thunderstorms around.

Tuesday June 16 — The first thing I saw as I picked up the *East Anglian* this morning, was that three inches of rain had fallen in Colchester and Sudbury last night. Houses were flooded and there were photos showing the water in people's homes — it seems that we are lucky to be living on a slight slope. There is so much water standing everywhere and we have had so many storms, it will take some time for the earth to settle down again. I had my friend, John, come to fix my outside lights; we had to wait until the robins had gone out of the shed before doing this, as some of the electric wire was connected into that building. This evening, a group of ladies from Barham Ladies Club came to visit the garden.

Wednesday June 17 — I went to Ipswich this morning to do my programme, then called at the Heath Road Hospital to see my sister, Pat, who has a bad back. There seems so much back trouble these days and one of the sisters in the hospital to whom I spoke, told me that it was one of the most common complaints. She did say that it is a pity that people never learn to bend properly when they pick things up, but I am afraid that we are all in such a hurry these days that we don't think to take this simple precaution.

I arrived home just in time to receive a coach-load of ladies from Kessingland W.I. and I was thankful that it was fine. Since tea, we have had another coach-load from Tendring, near Clacton — this too was a group of W.I. ladies. It has been quite a busy day today, but I am so glad that the weather was fine so that they could all have a good look around. After everyone had gone, I cut eighteen cabbages, ready to take to the W.I. market — they all seem to be coming on at once.

Thursday June 18 — A bonus with the weather today — the sun came out! I went to the market and the amount of produce we get in for sale is quite astonishing at times. It includes bedding plants, pot plants, vegetables, eggs, pickles and jams, cakes of every description and a wonderful assortment of crafts and there is always a long queue at Woodbridge market, waiting for the doors to open at ten o'clock.

The market only lasts an hour and a quarter and usually everything is sold out, but during that period there is still time to have a nice cup of coffee and a cake.

I didn't hang about long at Woodbridge after the market, but got home and cleared up a lot of my old spring cabbage leaves and stalks. I then singled the parsnips and planted out a row of Curly Kale, this is a super vegetable to have in the winter and I cannot understand why more people don't grow it. I did a lot of weeding and let my chicks out into the big run with my old hens, so that they could have a good run around. It really is marvellous to see how this old "banty" has mothered these chicks; there is an old saying that "banty hens make the best foster-mothers" and I certainly have proved this to be true, as far as this one is concerned. She is so protective and will soon fly at any of the other hens who dare to go near her babies. After tea, a party of ladies from Belstead, near Ipswich, came to see the garden.

Friday June 19 — Back to rain again! It was raining cats and dogs when I got up at six o'clock and it was really miserable until about 3.00 pm. I went to have coffee with the American lady, Mrs. Ray Wright, who lives in the old schoolhouse at Kettleburgh. The visit brought back so many memories of my school days. There has not been too much changed there; they still have what we called the big room and the little room plus they have added an extra room on the back of the building. Also, as the main building has such a high roof, half of it has been made into another bedroom, with a spiral staircase leading to this from the main room. It even has the old tarmac all round the building, which used to be our playground. I was fascinated to see how an old school could be made into living accommodation.

In the evening, I went to Ipswich to do my radio programme. Sudbury has had bad storms and flooding again, pour souls, to be flooded out twice in one week — how terrible!

Saturday June 20 — Hooray! I woke up to sunshine; I wonder, are we in for a better day. I did some weeding, but it is quite a problem with all this wet; the weeds seem to grow as fast as you pull them out. After lunch, I went to open a school fete in Ipswich, on the Chantry Estate and I won a lovely iced cake in a raffle; it really looked too good to eat. Sugar craft icing has really caught on over the years and you do see some cakes with the most beautiful designs on them. My brother agreed as well, that it was too good to cut so we decided, as it will be our church fete next week, we would give it as a prize or for a raffle, whichever the committee decided.

This evening, we had a bus load from Leigh-on-Sea in Essex, to visit the garden and, yes, you can guess — it was pouring with rain again all the evening.

Sunday June 21 — Another bonus with the weather today; perhaps because it is Father's Day or perhaps, as my diary says, "Summer begins — the longest day". Ruby and Pat, two friends from Norfolk, came over for the day and two coaches from the Peasenhall district also called in. It really is a treat to have a warm day. I also had more friends call round this evening and we sampled a glass or two of my rose-petal wine and also my gooseberry wine which I had strained earlier in the day. I know it is Sunday, but these jobs have to be done when I can fit them in.

Monday June 22 — It was a pleasant start to the morning but by eleven o'clock it was wet again. I begin to wonder whether we are ever going to get a continuous spell of fine weather.

However, I had a nice day as I went to an Old People's Home in Ipswich and cut the cake for the Anchor Group, apparently all over the country this is known as Anchor Week. I was given a very pretty pot plant in a basket and shown around this new home. While I was there, it was rather nice to be able to sit and chat to some of the old people. Unfortunately, I had to leave early as I knew that a coach load of disabled people were coming to visit the garden but by the time I got home, the rain was still pouring down and sadly, although the bus arrived, nobody could get out to look around. It is such a shame when people come out for the day and the weather turns out so bad.

This evening, I packed up a lot of copies of my book, "A Country Girl at Heart", ready to send off to the U.S.A. These should arrive in time for distribution at my lectures.

Tuesday June 23 — More rain — first thing this morning, I caught up with a lot of paperwork and also did some housework. Going outside into the garden I noticed that the fly had attacked my carrots, this is rather unusual as you don't normally expect this with all the wet weather which we have had. The rain eased off later in the day and I did some work in the greenhouse. I had a group of ladies from the Womens Institute from Stoke-by-Nayland and thankfully, the weather was fine for them.

Wednesday June 24 — After doing my radio programme in Ipswich, I went and had a look in some of the shops and managed to buy a navy-blue suit, ready for my trip in the autumn. I didn't linger long, however, as I had to get home to greet the first coach of the day which brought ladies from Great Blakenham then after tea, I had another coach, this time from Barningham near Bury St. Edmunds. It really was an enjoyable social evening. Strange too, I thought, how the weather always clears up later in the day.

We have had a stray peacock: this was in my neighbour's garden and he looked to be doing a lot of damage, eating the plants; so far, he has not ventured into my garden, I think that probably he has an idea that Sally would not make him welcome.

Thursday June 25 — Yes, I have got to say it again — another

HARVEST FESTIVAL AT HEMINGSTONE CHURCH

W. I. MARKLET STALLS

SALLY, MY DOG

COLOURFUL TREES IN THE U.S.A.

PUMPKINS IN THE U.S.A.

W. I. MARKLET STALLS

HOO CHURCH

HARVEST FESTIVAL AT LETHERINGHAM CHURCH

wet day! I went to Woodbridge early to get some paint; a friend is going to start work outside on my windows and also do some decorating indoors for me later, if the weather will let him.

Little Russell has chicken-pox but he doesn't seem to be too ill, I just hope that Sarah gets it so that they can get over it together.

I had a listener ring me today to say that he has no beans on his plants, although they flowered six weeks ago; why was this? One reason could be that, being so cold, there were no bees around to pollinate them. Many people have also lost their runner-beans again, one of the common complaints being that the seed is rotting in the ground. I put a tray full in my greenhouse for my neighbour, as rabbits had bitten all his off.

Ronnie was asked to work late again today as tar and chippings had been peeling off the roads which had only recently been resurfaced. We wondered what could have caused this; was it the wet?

I went and recorded two tapes for the programme "Morning is Broken", this is a daily religious spot on Radio Orwell and is broadcast fairly early in the morning.

Friday June 26 — Another damp day. My friend, George Woods, started painting outside the house; I just hope that the weather lets him get on with it as it is so annoying when you have to keep stopping and re-starting, with paintwork. I noticed that my summer cauliflowers had all started to burst, due to the wet weather; I cut nine large ones, some weighing over 4lb, and made a lot of mustard pickle, it is rather early, but at least they won't go to waste. I also managed to do a good old bake-up since it was a bit wet underfoot outside.

In the evening, I went to Ipswich to do the gardening programme and afterwards had a good rest before going early to bed.

Saturday June 27 — Raining early, and it is our Church Fete today; after a quick discussion with the Committee, we decided to hold it in the Village Hall. It went very well and we made £425, but there is not the same atmosphere as being out in the garden. Village fetes are not like they used to be and I suppose you can put it down to people having cars and televisions; the Annual Summer Fete used to be a highlight of the year, but not anymore, I am sorry to say!

By the evening, it was warm and humid, Ron dug up my spring cabbage bed and we planted celery plants where the cabbages had been while I did a little weeding, but my back is bad so I had to take it easy.

Sunday June 28 — Went to Hoo Church for the 8.30 early service and again the morning has turned out very warm and humid. I had a 'phone call when I got back, to say that my uncle, who lived in Saxmundham, had died. He will be missed as he was a good man, very clever; if you gave him a scrap of brass he could make almost anything from it.

This afternoon, we have had several visitors in the garden and I had friends in after tea, it made a nice change to spend a quiet evening together.

Monday June 29 — Very hot today; what a change from last week. I weeded the leeks and onions early on, but after eleven o'clock it was too hot to work outside; our English weather is unbelievable. I came inside the house, where it was cooler, and did some housework then wrote some letters.

On the whole, the garden is looking fine but I feel disappointed to see the carrots which have got the fly. I have to say that I have never seen them look this bad before but never mind, you have to take the rough with the smooth.

Tuesday June 30 — Another warm day. I went to Ipswich to record my radio programme today as I am going to Bressingham tomorrow. When I got home it was really too hot to do anything outside and I am not expecting any coach parties today, so I decided to take things easy. After tea, I strained four more gallons of gooseberry wine then, as the weather was cooler, I did a lot of weeding

In my little patio at the back of the house near the back door, the scent of the roses and honeysuckle are now at their best and in the evenings, with the blackbirds singing from the top of the television aerial, what more could one wish for, I ask?

Many supporters of the Ipswich Labour M.P. Mr. Ken Weetch, have felt sadness and regret that he lost his election campaign to a Mr. Michael Irvine, Conservative candidate, and that Mrs. Thatcher won her historic third term of government.

This June must rank as one of the most dreary and miserable months since records began as it rained on most days; in the Ipswich area, over eight inches of rain was recorded.

HINTS FOR JUNE

June is a month which can bring high temperatures but also some sharp showers. It is a very busy time in the flower and vegetable garden where things will happen very quickly. Sow biennials, like wallflowers, sweet williams, canterbury bells, evening prim-roses, honesty, bellis daisies, pansies and forget-me-nots and in the vegetable garden, autumn broccoli, calabrese, cabbage (Celtic January King) and swede. Now is the time to transplant early leeks, these need to be spaced 6 to 8 inches apart in rows 18 inches apart. I like to trim about two inches off the top of the leeks before planting as this seems to stop the birds pulling them from the holes. Stop cutting asparagus at the end of June and give them a good feed as you will need to build up the crowns for next year.

Tender annual climbers, such as cobaea standens, morning glory or impomoeas, and canary creeper (tropaeolum pereyrinum) can all be raised under glass. Watch out for the raspberry beetle as this will soon be about, so spray well with derris dust.

We often say "a good leak in June sets all things in tune" but, although June brings the longest days and the strongest sunshine, it is not often the warmest month of the summer. This is because the soil has not yet warmed up. Remember the old saying "the peasant longs for rain, the holidaymaker longs for sunshine, but God gives each what is best".

Houseplants can be put outside now but keep them in partial shade in a north-facing position and don't forget to give them water and food as well as removing any old leaves. Herbs should be growing well and are now at their best for drying or freezing. Pick the young fresh leaves of sage, thyme and fennel and dry them on trays in a cool oven, with the door left open. When dry and brittle, rub them down to fine crumbs then pack into small airtight bottles and store them in a dark cupboard. It is now that I pick my parsley and after washing and patting it dry, I pop it into small bags and put into the freezer. You will find that it is jolly handy for use in the wintertime.

If you have a small pool, you will notice that, as the warm weather comes, algae and blanket weed can become a problem and these need to be removed regularly. The green filaments can be collected, to some extent, by twisting a stick around in the water. I also use an old scrubbing brush around the sides of my pond. Oxygenating plants will help to keep the water well supplied with air and a fountain will do much to keep the oxygen levels high enough to prevent the fish from getting too warm.

Another job which my brother does in June, is to dig up the old spring cabbage bed and plant out a row of celery and a row of celeriac, this latter one is a fine vegetable and grows to about the size of a tennis ball — it is a good to use in salads and stews during the winter months.

COURGETTE OMELETTE

For each person you will need 2 eggs, about an ounce of cheese and 5 or 6 oz courgettes (when prepared for cooking). Cook the courgettes in a little butter or oil or just in its own juice, in a covered pan but do not let the liquid boil off at the end. Tip into a bowl, add the beaten eggs, grated cheese, salt and pepper (preferably black and freshly ground). Stir well and tip into a frying pan in which you have heated a little butter or oil. When it sets round the edges, loosen them and cover the pan — a plate upside-down will do if you have no lid. When the top is nearly set, in five or ten minutes depending on the size, put the pan under a hot grill to brown the top. (If your pan or it's handle won't stand up to this, just let it cook covered until set). Dish up hot, by itself or with vegetables or let it get cold, when it is excellent with salad, or of course, make a really big one and have it both ways.

July

WEDNESDAY JULY 1 — The month has come in with a nice warm day. I went to the Press Day at Bloom's of Bressingham. We had a tour of the nurseries and were taken round on Alan Bloom's train. It is remarkable what has been done on what was once wasteland, now turned into many beds of colourful herbaceous plants. We also went into Adrian Bloom's garden where there must be one of the most spectacular displays of conifers and heathers ever planted together in an English garden. We enjoyed a wonderful lunch which had been laid out in a marquee, and eventually I arrived home at a quarter to five, feeling exhausted. What a pleasure it had been, to see old and new friends and to walk among flowers on such a lovely sunny day.

In the evening, I had a coach party of visitors from near Colchester and they all told me how very much they had enjoyed looking round the garden.

Thursday July 2 — Another nice warm day but rather a sad one for me, as my uncle was buried this afternoon in Saxmundham Cemetery. My son, Allan, drove myself and Ronnie to the funeral where a lot of people had congregated to pay their last respects. He will be missed by many and as one friend at the church reminded us, "he was able to make a thing of beauty out of almost any piece of brass or wood". We got home at 4.30 pm. It seems strange, but whenever I go to a funeral now, it makes me think of the time when we filmed "Akenfield"— it is the only time when you meet all the relations at once!

97

I picked one of my strawberries today from the plants which I have grown in a forty-gallon barrel — the variety of this was Grandee and weighed some $2^1/_4$ oz. You may wonder how they are grown in a barrel; holes are cut alternately all the way round and I am able to plant more than three dozen plants in these holes. It is very similar to a strawberry barrel which you can buy from the garden centres, only this one is much bigger.

This evening I went to a Parish Council meeting and, as I had two parties of ladies, one from Framlingham and the other from Hintlesham, in to visit the garden, a friend came in to help Ronnie look after them. On leaving the garden, the parties were entertained by the Charsfield W.I. ladies who had prepared suppers at the village hall for forty-five people. This is where a fine village spirit is seen. The church ladies do cream teas for my afternoon visitors while the W.I. caters for some of my evening visitors, by arrangement. The result is that both groups add to their funds and their efforts support mine here in the "Akenfield" garden, which is open to the public for charity. We all help one another in Charsfield.

Friday July 3 — This morning I went to St. Audrys Hospital, as a retirement party was being held for one of the ladies from the Social Centre — Mrs. Whitsun. I had known Joan for a number of years. It was nice to go back and see so many old friends and talk over old times.

I arrived home in time to meet a Miss Jane Fearnley, who is writing a book on roses, she was anxious to see how I grow mine in a cottage garden. We spent a long time walking around while I pointed out to her the different varieties and explained my methods of growing them. Later in the afternoon a coach party from Harris's called in with visitors from London. Having said goodbye to these people, I then went to Ipswich and did my gardening programme.

Saturday July 4 — I got up early this morning to a day which is warm and fine and had a couple of hours working in the greenhouse before going up to Hoo Church where it is my turn to do the flowers. Coming back from church, I spent a bit more time in the garden before getting ready to go out to a concert at Ipswich Corn Exchange this evening. The concert was called "Suffolk Punch" and was held in aid of the National Children's Homes. My part was to do a reading from the book "Akenfield". There were several well-known personalities who all took their turn, either reading or singing, etc., all of whom gave their time free of charge. While in the waiting room, I sat with Bill Treacher who plays Arthur in the popular soap opera, Eastenders. He is a charming man and in our conversation he told how hard he has to work on the programme. Bill lives near Stowmarket but travels up to London most week-ends. The evening finished with some fine singing from the Olive Quantrill Singers. It was a fascinating evening and the only thing I could really find fault with, was that the Corn Exchange was so hot — we were all glad to come out into the cool air.

Sunday July 5 — It has still been very hot today. Because the area has a number of special events planned, we didn't have so many visitors, however, some friends did call in and brought me some strawberries.

An old, but dear friend, Clifford Arbon, called to see me. He is now over eighty years old but still rides his motor-cycle. Clifford loves to come and look round the garden, also to have a glass of home-made wine! A rather more peaceful day than usual.

Monday July 6 — I got up early and gave all my hanging baskets an extra watering — they do need it twice a day in this very hot weather. I made six pounds of strawberry jam and then, with another six pounds of strawberries which my neighbour brought, I made a gallon of wine.

A lady journalist came to see me this morning as she is going to write an article on the garden for one of the top magazines, *Homes & Gardens*, although it will not be included until next year. This afternoon I went to Melton to look after the grandchildren; Sarah has gone down with chicken-pox so we could not go out very far, at least she will get it over while she is young. This evening a coach load of visitors came from Felstead near Braintree.

Tuesday July 7 — It is still very warm, so I decided to go into Woodbridge early to do some shopping. Coming home, I fiddled about with some of my wine and also picked a lot flowers for drying; they do have to be picked as soon as they show the first signs of colour.

I have had four coach parties today, which put over eighty pounds in the charity box; one from Southend, a Mothers Union party; a British Legion outing from Capel St. Mary; a Harris coach from London and a W.I. party from Gipping near Stowmarket. In the evening, I had a 'phone call from America, asking me to do yet another extra talk— this will make fourteen in all. As you can guess , I was feeling rather used-up by the end of the day.

Wednesday July 8 — I got up early and did quite a few jobs as it looked like being a hot day. I went to Ipswich to do "Peggy's Patch" but didn't stay long as I always find it exhausting in the town when it is so hot. More coach parties today — one from a Church group in Ipswich and another coach-load of ladies from Scole, near Eye. After tea, the Mothers Union from Wenhaston came and held their meeting in the garden, there were only twenty-five of them so it was all quite comfortable. I made them tea but they had brought their own refreshments. They gave me a £5 garden token, which I thought was very kind of them.

Thursday July 9 — I went to the W.I. market then called in to see Jackie and the children. I was shocked to see poor little Sarah as she was now so ill with chicken-pox, covered from head to toe with spots, she even has them in her eyes — she certainly doesn't look like the little girl I know at all.

In the evening a coach party came from Thorpe-le-Soken near Clacton and after their visit to me they were given supper in the village hall by our W.I. members.

Friday July 10 — Got up early and went to Polstead to get some Black Morello cherries — they make a tasty wine. I also made a nice cherry brandy by putting the cherries into a large jar, after first pricking them, and then pouring a bottle of vodka or cheap brandy over them and adding a little sugar. The jar needs to be shaken quite often over a period of ten days and this will make a welcome drink for Christmas. Although the weather has been rather warm and humid today, I have had several visitors to the garden.

Jackie 'phoned to say that she had taken Sarah to see the doctor as she was so ill — poor little mite! This evening I have been to Ipswich for my gardening programme.

Saturday July 11 — This morning I went to the Ipswich Flower Show early — I am honoured to be their president, and while I was there, I judged the classes for cut flowers. The flower arrangement class was down this time as a number of ladies were involved with helping to do flowers for the Flower Festival at Ely Cathedral. After a busy day at the show, I arrived home at half past four and although I was tired I did a lot of weeding and dead-heading of flowers this evening; I also picked a lovely bunch of sweet peas. The garden is a haven of scent and colour at the moment, it really is an ideal time to walk around in the evening or first thing in the morning, to appreciate all the perfumes.

Sunday July 12 — Went to see little Sarah early today, thank God she is better but I have never seen a child with so many spots — in her hair, eyes and mouth; everywhere in fact.

We had a very busy day and Ron had to work hard trying to find room for the visitors to park their cars. I am amazed at how people will come out when it is so very hot. Claude and Iris called in during the evening but by the time they left about eleven o'clock I was 'out for the count'.

Monday July 13 — Went to work early in the garden this morning — with this sort of weather it is the only time that gardening can be done with any degree of comfort. However, Sally doesn't seem to worry too much about the weather so I took her for a walk just up the lane. Later on, I went to lunch with an old friend, Doris Fox. Over the years she has been very ill but she is a person who never complains. It was she who first taught me how to arrange flowers but in the years since I first knew her, I have learned so many other things.

When I arrived home David's wife, Norine, called and brought me some more strawberries so I will make them into jam for her. After tea, the Tangent Club from Ipswich came to visit the garden.

Tuesday July 14 — Another busy day with visitors — in all, four coaches. One from the London County Hall Horticultural Society, another from the Over 60's Club in Bury St. Edmunds while the other two were from the Ipswich area, the ladies from the St. John Ambulance and a party of W.I. ladies from Playford. I am glad that the weather was fine so that they saw the garden at its best. Fortunately, I had made scones early in the morning, just in case they were required so I was able to provide tea and scones for the London coach party.

Between the coach parties, my neighbour let me go to pick some raspberries from his garden and I was able to gather eight pounds — a good ending to a good day.

Wednesday July 15 — I went to do my programme at Radio Orwell then as there were one or two sales advertised, I went to do some more shopping for my forthcoming trip to America. I arrived home at about two o'clock, just before a party from Pettistree W.I. After the visitors had gone, I racked and strained some of my wine. The cherry wine which I dealt with still seemed to be active so I decided to add a few raspberries and do a second take — we shall have to wait and see how it turns out! For a change we have had one or two showers today.

Thursday July 16 — The rain simply fell down all morning, but it came just right for the garden. Fortunately, it stopped after lunch so the party from the Mothers Union from Aldeburgh were able to walk round the garden; there were twenty members and I was able to serve them with tea and scones.

An exciting letter arrived today from the editor of the *East Anglian Daily Times*, asking me to write a weekly article for their Woman's Page starting in September.

Friday July 17 — Woke up to rain again this morning so I did a lot of housework and wrote my gardening notes for the week. The rain cleared by lunchtime although the wind began to get stronger and started blowing the baskets about. As they are now so big, I went out and took some of them down. After I had done the gardening programme in Ipswich, I managed to pick and shell eight pounds of broad beans for the freezer.

Saturday July 18 — What a morning — the Heavens just opened up again. It's such a shame as there are so many shows on this week-end, in fact, I suppose this is the most popular week-end of the summer season in East Anglia for summer Shows. I went and opened the Melton fete — this was in aid of the Under 5's Toddler Group, then I went on to present a cup at the Co-operative Horticultural Show, as once more I am honoured to be their President. As I came home I called at the market and managed to buy some cheap peaches; these I shall make into wine. I made five pounds of raspberry and redcurrant jelly and then, after tea, went to Melton to baby-sit with Russell and Sarah; I was glad to sit and rest after a hectic day.

Sunday July 19 — Thundering and lightning early this morning and the rain absolutely fell down until about eleven o'clock, when the skies cleared. The garden was opened in aid of Suffolk Conservation and we managed to take £40 — this was not bad considering the awful weather of this morning. I was able to pick three pounds of raspberries off my bushes in between the showers

— it is one blessing that the foliage and plants soon dry out in the summer, after these heavy showers. It kept fine until about five o'clock and then it rained cats and dogs again! In the evening, I lit a small fire as it was so chilly and decided to have an early night.

Monday July 20—Once more, it poured with rain this morning but it was fine by lunchtime. I strained the raspberry and cherry wine, tidied the house, then went and looked after the grandchildren again.

I took them for a nice walk, on to Melton playing field and round into the wood. There are several pleasant walks around there and I can understand why the local people don't want the land sold for building, as so often happens in our villages nowadays.

This evening, I had a party visit the garden from Southwold; it managed to keep fine while they were there but just as they left, the Heavens opened up again.

Tuesday July 21 — The repetition in this diary, of wet weather notes may seem tedious and even depressing to some readers, but the rain is an undoubted fact of life and we country people are, despite our moans, fairly resigned to it, probably realising its benefits more directly than do the townsfolk. However, thank goodness, today it did stop around two o'clock; this was just as a party from the Shottisham Over 60's Club came to look round the garden. The Church ladies kindly gave them tea at the end of their visit.

In the evening, the W.I. from Elmsett came to see the garden; for a change, it was a nice evening although it got dark quite early. I cannot understand why we seem to get these dark evenings so often nowadays at the height of summer, by 8.30 pm sometimes its almost impossible to see to do much outside.

This has been one of those days too, when my telephone never stopped ringing. One of the calls was from a lady enquiring whether it was time to pickle walnuts, and I replied yes! Another caller asked how much water to add to six pounds of gooseberries when making jam. You just would not believe some of the questions I get asked, but as long as I am not required to be a Marriage Guidance counsellor, I don't mind, as it is satisfying to be able to help people with genuine needs.

Wednesday July 22 — Went off to Ipswich to do my radio programme this morning — in steady rain! This weather is getting not only boring, but very serious now as it has been wet again for most of the day, on and off. This would be the day too, when I had my party from Stow Lodge Hospital—poor dears, the rain just fell down when they left the coach, in their wheelchairs. They stayed in my garage for a while but the staff who accompanied them decided that unfortunately, they would have to take them back to the hospital. I felt so sorry for them as this is one outing they look forward to, but sadly my house is not equipped to cope with wheelchairs.

After tea, I had a small group from the Ipswich Co-op Club here — they did just manage to walk around between the heavy showers. Later in the evening some of the ladies from the village came in and we held a meeting to decide how to run the Over 60's Christmas meal this year. This party was instituted many years ago and there are still dedicated ladies who get together every year to ensure that everything goes well on the day.

Thursday July 23 — Dare I say it again — the rain started at lunchtime and kept going on for the rest of the day. I shall soon need over-boots to get into my chicken run, the poor birds are up to their necks in mud. I have never seen the run so muddy in the middle of summer. Thank goodness my neighbour lets me open the gate so that they can run into his orchard, but sadly, you won't get any eggs if the hens are cold and have got muddy feet.

A party came from Aldeburgh W.I. to visit the garden this evening and they managed to walk around between the storms.

Again it was dark early — it is hard to believe that it is still summer and I grow more convinced than ever that the weather, if not the season, is seriously out of order.

Friday July 24 — I got up early and decided to have a really good baking day, making up batches of cheese rusks and scones, ready for Sunday teas; I also cleaned up the house as I couldn't do much outside because of the pouring rain.

My neighbour brought me some more raspberries — I do hope the fruit will keep long enough for us to get it into our preserving pans; all this rain is bad for soft fruit and a lot of the soft fruit farmers look likely to have a very bad year.

My brother is getting very worried as he wants to cut the grass, but with all the wet it is impossible to use the mower.

Saturday July 25 — A better day — and what a relief, as today the Village Flower Show was held. As I have been so busy these past few weeks I am afraid that I did not enter anything this year, as it does take time to get entries ready. As it happened, I was also due to judge at Melton Flower Show, then on to open a similar Flower Show at Great Cornard so, despite having no part in our own Flower Show, my hands have not been idle today. At both the events, I was given a very warm welcome and in spite of the bad weather, they had many stalls set out on Great Cornard playing field, together with a car-boot sale. I bought eights sets of home-made wine kits for £1 — I thought this was a good buy, somebody had obviously become fed up with making wine. I arrived back home at half past four and after tea, we managed to pick some peas and beans. We also stayed outside weeding, until ten o'clock. I came in and had what we would call in this part of the country, "a funny turn" — when I came to, I found myself lying on the floor. However, after sitting down for a while, I soon felt better; I expect it was the result of all this rushing and tearing around.

Sunday July 26 — Went to Hoo Church for the early service, then I got the garage ready for teas and coffee as the garden was open today for our Over 60's summer party. Two coach loads arrived and kept us really "on the hop", although we had four other ladies helping with the refreshments. We provided tea and cakes at 50p per head and, with admissions, at the end of the day we had made £241. Ron and I had our "lunch" after 7 pm and by bedtime, I was all-in.

Our local paper, *The East Anglian Daily Times*, reports that we have had the worst wet weather in the whole of Britain, over the last nine days — I wonder if it is all down to St. Swithin's?

Monday July 27 — I woke up early, still feeling rather tired and soon after breakfast, drove to Woodbridge with the results of the Flower Show, for the *East Anglian*; then I tidied up the house after yesterday's invasion, sorting out cups and plates and putting them away. I had some trouble with my gooseberry wine — it was not fermenting in the wine shed because it was too cold so I had to put it in the airing cupboard. This is quite unusual because other years, the shed has been so warm that the wine has been quite happy to work in there.

A party came from the Great Bromley Garden Club this evening; thank goodness it was fine for them but, once again, the light went very quickly.

Tuesday July 28 — My friend, Perry, picked me up early this morning and took me to gather some loganberries and red currants at Sudbourne near Orford. The fruit was really first class and I came home and made ten pounds of redcurrant jelly and four gallons of loganberry wine, the remainder of the fruit I put in the freezer.

I had some friends call unexpectedly, so we went in and had some coffee, this gave me the time for a bit of rest and a chat, they came from Lakenheath so we don't see each other very often. Three coach parties also arrived on schedule, one from Layer-de-la-Haye, the Over 60's Club, one from Sicklesmere W.I. and my regular one from Harris's of London — another busy day.

Wednesday July 29 — What a day! the promise of good weather over the past few days hasn't continued, as there was a heavy thunderstorm which started at about three o'clock this morning and carried on until nine o'clock. Because of the dampness outside, I spent most of the morning doing correspondence and odd jobs around the house. After lunch, a party came from the Clacton British Legion, to look round the garden and although it was fine while they were there, the rain started again soon after they had left. Another party of W.I. ladies came — they were not as fortunate and because it was raining so hard they could not even get out of the bus, so I went in with them and gave them a talk about the garden instead and they promised that they would come back another time. Between the showers I did manage to gather some peas, broad beans and dwarf beans, so in the evening I set-to and prepared a lot of these for the freezer.

Thursday July 30 — W.I. market this morning, after which I called in to see Jackie and the grandchildren. Happily, the weather was a bit better today. In the afternoon, a group of W.I. ladies from the Martlesham Institute came and they were followed by a party from a church in Ipswich. I also had the W.I. from Swaffham in Norfolk, some ladies from the village helped me to serve them with tea and scones and we were able to make another £70 for our Over 60's fund. By eight o'clock it was getting dark and as it would have been impossible for anybody to look round in the fading light, I was relieved that no more visitors turned up.

Friday July 31 — Another fairly early start for me today. I left home by 8.30 am to go and start the judging for Floral Ipswich — the garden competitions. We started at 9.15 and finished at five o'clock. During the day, we visited thirty gardens in addition to Old People's Homes. We did stop for an hour at lunchtime, and this was needed for the day has been warm and humid. On finishing the judging, I went on to Radio Orwell where I did the gardening programme. I felt dead-beat when I got home at half past eight; in fact its been a long time since I have felt so tired.

July has been a very busy month for me, in more ways than one. This must surely have been one of the wettest summers on record and many of the flowers have been spoilt before they even came into bloom and yet the visitors have still continued to turn up. Locally, Ipswich is still in a state of shock at the news that the 118 year old firm of Ransomes and Rapiers, one of the town's largest engineering works, is to close with the loss of four hundred jobs.

HINTS FOR JULY

Some people say that June is for roses, but July will see roses, roses all the way and every gardener has a soft spot for this most delightful of blooms. Rose water was known as early as 140BC and it is still used for many purposes, including flavouring as well as perfume. A little, mixed with glycerine, makes a pleasant hand lotion, a teaspoonful in whipped cream is lovely with strawberries and a teaspoonful or more gives a delicate flavour to sponge cakes or ice cream. Deep-scented red roses are the best because they have a strong perfume and colour and I use these for making my rose-petal wine. Rose vinegar will give an extra bite to a fruit salad, and to make this, half fill a jar with rose petals, cover with best white wine vinegar and steep for twenty-four hours, preferably in the sun, and then strain.

If the weather gets very warm, shade fuchsias to prevent the buds from dropping and the leaves from scorching. Cut hedges, such as holly, beech hornbeam and yew. Privet hedges may need cutting for the second time this year but do use a good pair of sharp shears.

After the raspberries have finished fruiting, remove the old fruited canes or thin them out, leaving only the strongest canes. Clear soil around the onion bulbs to aid ripening and allow the tops to bend over naturally as they are still growing.

Geranium cuttings root very easily now, either outside in pots or in open ground in sheltered borders. You may think that this is early but there is no need to spoil the displays, just take nonflowering shoots 4 - 5 inches long, cut below a node or joint then plant, using a mixture of half peat and half sharp sand. Geranium seeds may be sown at the end of the month and gardeners, even without heated propagators, should get good plants before the winter comes in and ones which will bloom earlier next summer.

Propagate border carnations and pinks now, by the layering method — find a nice shoot close to the soil then, with a sharp knife, make an incision along the stem about one inch (2.5 cm) and using a hairpin or piece of wire, pin the stem down in to a pot of potting compost buried in the soil. After about four weeks, when it should have rooted sufficiently, simply sever it from the parent plant.

Spinach needs sowing in July so that it is ready for winter use and carry on feeding tomatoes and take out side shoots. Runner beans are thirsty plants and in case we get a dry spell, give them a good mulch.

Now is the time to pick lavender for making in to bags. The stalks should be cut full length and just before the flowers are fully open, usually about the first week in July. Hang them up to dry, then, with the fingers, rub the blossom free from the stalks and this can then be put into bags. Talking of lavender, there is an old wives tale which suggest that primulas and yellow crocuses, which are elsewhere attacked by birds, are left untouched when grown beside a lavender hedge.

CHERRY AND BRANDY PIE

Pastry
8oz plain flour
Pinch of salt
4½ oz butter
5oz caster sugar
1 egg yolk
2 tablespoons water

Filling
2lb stoned cherries
milk and caster sugar
    for glazing
2 tablespoons cherry
    brandy or brandy
3 tablespoons double
    cream

Make up dough and knead lightly until smooth. Put into a floured plastic bag and chill for at least 30 minutes. Fill a 1½ pint pie dish with stoned cherries, sprinkle with extra sugar and clot with ½oz butter. Roll out pastry and cover dish of cherries, making a couple of slits in the top to let out the steam, brush with milk and caster sugar. Bake in a moderately hot oven 400°F or 200°C, Gas Mark 6, for 20 minutes then reduce heat to 375°F Gas Mark 5 for another 20 minutes until pastry is golden brown. Remove pie and cut neatly round the lid of the pie, lift off carefully and pour cherry brandy and cream over the fruit, Replace pastry lid, dredge with caster sugar and return to the oven for 5 minutes. Serve hot with whipped or clotted cream.

CHERRY BRANDY
1lb Morello Cherries; 4oz sugar; 1 bottle brandy or 1 bottle vodka
Place cherries, sugar and brandy in a jar, shaking occasionally. Keep for six months if possible.

August

SATURDAY AUGUST 1 — What a treat today; I didn't have to go out so I gave the house a good turn-out in readiness for two friends from Birmingham, who are coming to stay. I managed to cut a lot of dried flowers and hang these up in my wine shed, but it is unfortunate that this year, the wet weather has spoiled a lot of my dried material.

Ronnie and I managed to do a lot of weeding this afternoon. It has been an awful problem this year, the "unwanted" plants have grown quicker than the plants we set out! It was also Monewden Church Fete this afternoon; thank goodness they had a fine day.

Sunday August 2 — We had the garden open for the St. John Ambulance Brigade; it was a nice bright day and over two hundred people came in. The Brigade always sends two members of their staff for this day, this relieves Ronnie and myself considerably. They took £100 on the gate, which is a good help to their funds.

I learnt today of the death of a local fruit farmer, Mr. Tony Youngman; he was such a kind man and always had a smile and a joke for everyone and I am sure that the employees on the farm were devastated, as he was not an old man, although he had been very ill for the last few months. I think the entire village of Charsfield are going to miss him. It makes one realise what a tremendous blessing good health is.

Some friends came round in the evening and we had a good chat about making wine and jam etc.

Monday August 3 — A nice bright day again and I went to Charsfield Hall this morning and collected eighteen pounds of blackcurrants, I thought they were quite reasonable at 40p per pound, as they were ready picked. When I got home I started three gallons of wine off, after which I took some to my friend, Iris, who lives in Wickham Market and from there, I went on to look after my little grandchildren until late afternoon. I arrived home just in time to welcome another Harris's coach party.

As we were not expecting any visitors this evening, I had a session putting away all my jams and jellies. You may think this amusing — I put them up in my bedroom where I have a large built-in cupboard, which I use for storage. How I wish that I had got a large pantry, like we used to have in the olden days, but as my boys tell me, if I didn't store so many things like papers and books and clutter up the place generally, I would have more shelf space. One day, they will have a "blitz" clearing out this house — when I pass on!

Tuesday August 4 — Made an early start in the greenhouse, sorting out, dead-heading and taking some cuttings. The first coach party of the day arrived quite early, this was from Combs near Stowmarket. Soon after lunch, the second coach arrived from Walberswick and after the ladies had wandered round the garden, I made them some tea. It has been quite a busy day, one way and another, as I also had a coach party from Leiston in the evening. After this visit, our W.I. ladies gave them supper in the village hall.

I have noticed that the nights start to pull in now; by nine o'clock it is really dark.

Wednesday August 5 — This morning, I went to Ipswich early as I had to collect the ticket for my flight to America. I also had a look round the shops for some more clothes; they are all very expensive and anyway, I am not very keen on shopping for dresses and coats — I would much rather see what is new in the gardening world. Before leaving Ipswich, I went on to do my programme, "Peggy's Patch" then I called to see David and Norine. They are in the middle of changing houses but my word, how the prices go up, it seems thousands of pounds each week. It is an awful problem for young people today, who are trying to buy their own property.

I got back home in time for a coach load of ladies who came from Stanway near Colchester then, in the evening, another party from the W.I. at Roach Vale near Bury St. Edmunds.

Thursday August 6 — Another bright day so I took the opportunity to wash my car, by the look of the dust and grime on it, it should have been done days ago but this is one of the jobs which I have to do when I can find the time. Another task which needed doing was cleaning the windows and although this is not one of my favourite occupations, I set to with a will. By half-past four, despite the fine start to the day, the heavens opened and the rain fell solidly for an hour, I thought to myself, this is what happens when I have a cleaning session! Soon after tea, a party of ladies from Clacton-on-Sea W.I. and one from the W.I. in Ipswich came; they managed to walk around the garden, but they were all saying how cold it was, and if I am truthful, I felt much the same. After they had gone, I came in and lit a fire, it was quite cosy, then during the evening, I racked off my blackcurrant wine. Before I realised it, it was time for bed and sometimes I wonder just where the days go to.

Friday August 7 — Did a lot of baking today, making one hundred scones, shortbread and cheese rusks ready for teas on Sunday. I also gave my bedrooms a good clean and hoover and sorted out a lot of clothes which I no longer wear, so that I could take them along to the Oxfam shop. I went into Ipswich earlier than usual today, to look round the shops and managed to get myself a navy suit. After doing the radio programme for gardeners,

I returned home and later in the evening, managed to answer some of my mail.

Saturday August 8 — I woke up with the sun streaming into my bedroom; once we get over these heavy summer showers and storms, the weather soon clears and the sun is quite warm. I did a lot of washing, then had the rest of the day weeding in the garden. I singled out three rows of carrots, planted some lettuce plants and cut down all the old delphiniums and climbing sweet peas from behind the wine shed.

Came in at half-past nine and although I felt rather tired, I finished off some ironing then had a bath and got to bed at 11.30.

Sunday August 9 — I did a terrible thing this morning — overslept, and so did not go to church. The weather started off nice and bright, but by late morning the clouds began to build up and by two o'clock, the rain has begun to fall. By late afternoon, it was bucketing down again. I made tea in the garage, and in spite of the weather, we took £40 — this was in aid of the Historic Churches and the garden is open on their behalf all this week. By six o'clock, it was raining so hard that we gave up, came in, and had a nice cup of tea ourselves then had a restful evening. As I sat with my feet up, I thought back to this day a year ago when David and Norine were married; what a contrast in the weather, as it was such a lovely day on that happy occasion.

Monday August 10 — I got up quite early and made a start on writing my articles for September. I always feel I can write better in the early hours rather than late at night. I spent all the morning writing, in between 'phone calls — its times like these when I almost wish that I didn't have a 'phone.

As Allan, Jackie and the grandchildren are on holiday this week, I didn't need to go to Melton, babysitting. I put a lot of runner beans in the freezer; this took quite a time.

This evening, I went out with our W.I. to visit the lovely Constable country. We were met at Flatford Mill and taken to see where John Constable was born, and we also visited Dedham and East Bergholt where we inspected the famous bell cage in the churchyard. Afterwards, the ladies of Stratford St. Mary gave us supper. We got home at half-past ten and we all agreed that it had been a very enjoyable evening, certainly for me, it was a change to visit another Institute.

Tuesday August 11 — Another busy day with visitors, I had over one hundred people at the garden and I think that the pleasant sunshine accounted for this number. I had a coach party from Hopton Over 60's Club and many people came in cars. During the day, I also managed to pick a few more dried flowers as well as making six pounds of Early Rivers plum jam, then in the evening, my neighbour let me go and gather the last of his blackcurrants. I think I shall make a good quantity of tarts and put them in the freezer. Before bedtime, the rain began to fall again and I feel very sorry for farmers as the corn is beginning to go very black in some places and from my window, it is possible to see wheat which has this black "soot" on it — this is a disease which affects corn when it is standing in the wet too long.

Wednesday August 12 — The promise of a better day, and by late morning the air was full of the hum of combines working; at least the men are trying to make the best of the weather.

I went to Ipswich and saw a dressmaker as I have a dress to be altered. I also bought a pair of sandals and then lost them, I just cannot think where; whether they slipped off my basket or whether I left them somewhere else, I just don't know but either way, that was a waste of twenty–six pounds.

Having been to the Radio Station to do "Peggy's Patch", I called to see a friend who was in hospital, before coming home. This afternoon, I picked ten pounds of runner beans, some of which I put in the freezer although there is a limit to how much you can freeze, anyhow, I don't think runner beans freeze that well, in fact I prefer dwarf beans — mind you, I can always take them to the W.I. market. After tea, a party of ladies came from the Tunstall Ladies Group to look round the garden. By 8.30 pm, we had to pack up in the garden because it was getting so dark.

Thursday August 13 — I went to the W.I. market and took my runner beans together with eight bunches of lovely dahlias, some parsley and swiss chard. Runner beans were selling for 50p per pound — what a price, but the ladies from the market told me that at Marks & Spencer in Ipswich, they were 95p per pound!

Allan and Jackie called in with the children; the rain had sent them home early from the seaside. It was lovely to have them for a few hours, especially as it had not been planned. After they left the rain cleared up and I was able to take a lot more cuttings from greenhouse plants and shrubs. My brother Ronnie has been at home all day, with a tummy upset — I must say it is rather unusual for him to have a day off, so he must have felt ill.

Friday August 14 — Today has been marked as "One day for Life — Search '88". The idea is for people to take a photograph and send it, together with £1, in aid of Cancer Research. There will no doubt be many people all over England, taking photos today. The time of the day when the actual photo was taken, had to be noted and I went up to Mr. Freeman's farm at Bredfield at half-past nine this morning and took some lovely country farm shots. Ronnie told me of a field of corn at Pettistree which had been cut and stood in the old stooks, just like we used to see them when we were children so I went along and took a photo of that as well. Afterwards, I did my gardening notes for the week then went on to Radio Orwell.

Saturday August 15 — A warm day for a change — Ronnie and I went over to Allan's, as he was moving a lot of old rubbish from the bottom of his garden and had hired a little lorry for the day, so was glad of our help.

When we got home I baked some buns and scones as I

expect to be busy tomorrow, then after tea, we spent time tidying up the garden, weeding and trimming back some of the shrubs which were hanging over the pathways.

Sunday August 16 — What a pleasant day — the sun was really warm for the start of our special week in support of the National Garden Scheme. We were very busy with visitors and I was kept on the hop, making tea and orange squash and answering questions. My friend, Sheila, came to help, for which I was very thankful. I also had a Harris's coach party and they were pleased to have refreshments when they arrived. If only we had a little tea-room nearby, it really would be a godsend for the visitors. Despite the wet weather we have had, the baskets dry out very quickly so Ronnie is kept busy with the watering-can. At the end of a busy day, I was glad to sit down and rest.

Monday August 17 — After I had tidied up the house and generally cleaned up, I went and looked after the grandchildren. Although it wasn't exactly fine, it wasn't too bad and we went for a walk through Melton woods — I always think that it is such a pretty place and always full of interest.

In the evening I had friends call to see me about doing the flowers for their daughter's wedding, to be held on the 29th of this month. Today's weather has gradually got worse and it is now raining heavily again, so I am off to bed early.

Tuesday August 18 — Thank goodness, today started off much better, at least, the sun is shining. Throughout the morning quite a number of casual visitors called to look at the garden, then after lunch, a party came from St. Audry's Hospital at Melton. These ladies usually come once a year to have tea in the garden and although it is only a small party, I think they look forward to coming out and to having a home-made cake and a cup of tea.

This was the first free night we have had for a few weeks so I took the opportunity to make some jam. Ronnie took up some potatoes and we noticed that they were full of slugs, again this is another consequence of all the wet weather and we shall have to get them all up before long.

Wednesday August 19 — The sun came out after a dull start. I went to Ipswich then, on my return, gave a welcome to a coach load of ladies from Hatfield Peverel. One of these ladies was one hundred years old — I think she must be the oldest person we have ever had round the garden. The organiser had told me previously that she was coming with the group, so I had cut a bunch of flowers and made them into a spray, to give to her. She was amazing, so fit and full of life, it was a real joy to meet her.

Another coach party of ladies came this evening, these were from the Salvation Army in Ipswich. The ladies from our church catered for both parties so they were kept busy.

News of a horrifying event came in today — a man in Hungerford, Berkshire went on the rampage killing 14 people and wounding 14 more before killing himself. This must be one of the worst killings ever to happen in England — what terrible times we are living in. It makes one glad to be living here quietly in the country, although nowhere seems really safe nowadays.

Thursday August 20 — At the W.I. Market today one lady told me that she had noticed that runner beans were £1.12 in an Ipswich supermarket — fancy paying that price I thought. While in the area I called in to see Jackie, then went on to collect some flowers for a wedding on Saturday.

This afternoon a small party of male patients from St. Audry's Hospital came and I gave them tea in the garden, Sheila came and helped me out and for this I was grateful. In the evening a group from the Ipswich Aviation Club paid a visit to the garden and after they had left I started to make up some baskets and table arrangements ready for the wedding. The couple who are getting married — Alan Lee and Annette Vernon, were both disc jockeys at Radio Orwell.

I notice that the wheat field at the front of the house has been cut today.

Friday August 21 — The day started very warm and humid. I loaded up my car with flowers and containers and made my way to the Roman Catholic Church at Stowmarket as I had to do the flowers for the whole church for the wedding. It was so hot and I had a thumping headache, but I managed to have them finished by half-past four, then, on the way home I left the table arrangements at the Marlborough Hotel. Then it was back to Ipswich in the evening in time for the radio programme.

At about half past ten this evening we had a thunderstorm — undoubtedly this was the reason for my headache during the day.

After the hectic day it was good to get to bed and rest.

Saturday August 22 — What contrasts we are getting in our weather! Small wonder that the British country-folk pay it so much attention.

Today began with pouring rain! I went off to Alan and Annette's wedding at about a quarter to eleven. The rain was absolutely "bucketing" down during the service so it was impossible to take any photographs outside. However I was pleased with the flowers in the church, and so many people came up to thank me for arranging them, the colour scheme was lemon, white and green, and the Roman Catholic church at Stowmarket, being quite modern, had been a real challenge — fitting the flowers in with the severe style of the building.

From the church we went on to Ipswich, where a lovely reception was held at the Marlborough Hotel — arriving there in the middle of a terrible thunderstorm, but, once the guests were inside the weather was forgotten. I arrived home at 4.30 and had a nice surprise as Iris and Claude called round to see me. Whilst we were talking I had a phone call from Allan at Melton to say that a hail storm had hit the Woodbridge area, and to ask if I could go over to help them clear up the mess. We all piled into my car and drove over — and what a sight! I had never seen anything like it. Hailstones as large as bantams eggs were piled up everywhere and the roads were such a mess with leaves and broken branches all over the place, it was such a job to drive through them. As we got out of the car we noticed that a mist had formed giving the whole place the appearance of a ghost town in some nightmarish film. Jackie and Allan had managed to mop up the water, although the hailstones which had come down the chimney, gathering soot on the way, had made a horrible mess on the carpet. The children, who couldn't see the distressing side of the situation, were so pleased to tell me that they had black stones coming down the chimney, bless their hearts! Walking round to the back of the garden, I could have cried when I saw the greenhouse all smashed up and the hanging baskets dangling from bare threads.

This was the first time in many years that I had seen Allan shed a few tears, in fact since he was a child, and now, only due to the state of his car which had been left standing outside; it looked as though someone had just gone over it, banging with a hammer, I hate to think what the insurance company will say.

When we returned home we discovered that there had been only a little rain at Charsfield; it seemed unbelievable how so much damage had been caused in one small area only of the county while most of us had come off "scot-free".

Sunday August 23 — A much warmer day, and as I woke up I couldn't help thinking how lucky I was to escape the storm — the damage which it would have done in the garden just doesn't bear thinking about.

Today the garden has been open in aid of the Red Cross, and although we did not take as much as last year, £67 went in to their funds — I wonder if some people thought that we had been hit by the hail storm and because of this had not come.

Today we have been allowed to park on one of Mr. Kitson's fields, this has been a great help, and a gesture which we appreciated.

After tea, as if to round off the day, would you believe, it started to rain again.

Monday August 24 — I had the manuscript for my next book back for the second time for checking so I spent this morning and much of this evening going through it. It is a difficult job reading it word by word, but it has to be done. Although the rain started during the early afternoon, I did manage to get my washing dry. I am not used to being quite as inactive as I have been today, in fact I felt rather guilty, as I have spent most of the time reading.

Tuesday August 25 — Yet again we woke up to rain. I went to Woodbridge to post my manuscript back, then went on to Notcutts as they were giving me a quantity of catalogues to take to the U.S.A. After I arrived home some friends called from Ipswich, and they took me to the local pub for lunch. After they left I managed to make twelve pounds of plum chutney.

Apparently some places are becoming flooded with all the rain we are having — today it has just poured down for most of the time. As I look out of my front window I can see a couple of farmers looking at their corn, it must be an awful worry as part of the field is standing in water.

Wednesday August 26 — Went and did my programme for the radio, then on to Stowmarket to take all the flowers out of the church; I got back to welcome a party of 40 ladies from a church group in Weeley near Clacton. I was glad that the rain held off while they were there, but after they had left it fell down and has done so for the remainder of the day. Ron tells me that the corn on the field opposite is shooting — no wonder the farmer looked worried when I saw him yesterday. Later in the afternoon I went to Kettleburgh and Letheringham and took photos of the floods, much of the low-lying meadows are under water — I even saw allotments submerged as I drove home from Stowmarket.

In the evening I made some plum jam and managed to pick a few dahlias — in between the showers — for the W.I. market tomorrow.

Thursday August 27 — Today it really is cold. I went and helped at the market taking swiss chard, parsley and my flowers. From there I went on to see Jackie and the children. When I got home I packed three parcels of books etc. for the U.S.A. Needless to say it has been drizzling with rain all day which has seemed to make the cold even worse, in fact a report on the local radio during the day said that this was one of the coldest August days on record in the county — 52°F and 11°C.

This evening I went and helped decorate two windows in Melton old church for their Flower Festival, then came home and prepared some foliage ready for a wedding at Dallinghoo. Today was the first day since we opened the garden for the season that we have had no visitors.

Friday August 28 — I made an early start in Dallinghoo church as I had to arrange the flowers for five windows, and four pedestals together with twelve baskets to go on the pew ends, then there were small vases for the altar and war memorial. It was getting late in the afternoon before I finished, then when I arrived home there was a Harris's coach party from London. Eventually I was able to get off to Ipswich for the radio gardening programme, and got back home at about eight o'clock, when I was glad to sit down to sort out some mail and look at the local paper.

Saturday August 29 — Another miserable day, but I cheered up at the prospect of going to judge at the Kettleburgh Show. I wonder what my grandfather would have said were he alive today, as this was his home village. He was a gardener himself and a great man for the Shows, I am sure I get some of my talent from him. I thought that this was a good Show for a village and there were some fine vegetables exhibited.

After lunch I helped Ronnie to do some weeding, and we managed to stay outside until half past eight. I picked a lot of runner beans and tomatoes, then went in and cut up some red cabbage for pickling.

Sunday August 30 — The garden was open today for the Haemophilia Fund. We were very busy — a bus load turned up at half-past one, and altogether throughout the day we took £115 on the gate, with another £57 coming from a stall and a further £30 on teas. It has been a really pleasant day, for a change, and it is always rewarding to see so many friends who come back year after year to see and enjoy the garden.

Monday August 31 — Today being the last public holiday before Christmas (Goodness Gracious!) I was quite busy with visitors, but I managed to persuade Ron to have a day off to go fishing. This is a hobby he enjoys, but seldom makes time for these days. He doesn't like to leave me to cope alone with crowds of people in the garden. However I was glad he went off to do just as he pleased, especially when it turned out such a lovely warm and sunny day.

We had a dramatic incident here, though, during the afternoon, a young chap from Debach had an accident with his car only a few yards away, on the corner just below our lane. Thank goodness neither he or his passengers were badly hurt and we were able to help them pull themselves together with cups of tea.

This corner in Charsfield has been notorious for accidents over the years — so many drivers take it too fast. But most people drive too fast nowadays, especially in the narrow country lanes which are so much a part of the old-world charm of our Suffolk villages.

I suppose that August will go down as being one of the wettest months on record — as long as I live I don't want to see another summer like this one; river banks bursting, and hail storms with hail as large as eggs. Two inches of rain fell in forty-five minutes in one area, and in Chelmsford policemen swam to cars to make sure that no one was trapped inside. I think these events even shook Ronnie, as he said that he would never forget the damage done by the ice in the hail storm. August, too, will be remembered for the terrible killing and wounding of the people in Hungerford by the deranged gunman, Michael Ryan.

HINTS FOR AUGUST

August is the time to enjoy the garden, with its show of flowers and produce from the vegetable plot but, as always with gardening, there are some jobs which need doing to ensure the continuity of future crops. As the earlier vegetables, like peas and lettuces, are finished, dig and fertilize the ground ready for re-planting. Sow spring cabbage, one of the best varieties to appear over the years is one called "Spring Hero", which makes a round cabbage weighing four pounds and over and which matures early.

Wallflower seedlings which were sown in May in the nursery bed, should now be transplanted into rows so that the plants are sturdy before planting out into beds later in the year, ready for the spring flowering. Carry on picking everlasting flowers, such as helichrysum, acroclinium, statice and moluccella (Bells of Ireland), also grasses and seed pods for use in winter bouquets. Remember to cut them just as the bloom shows colour, then tie into small bunches and hang up to dry in a cool, airy position — don't lay them out on the greenhouse bench.

Make the most of soft fruits, red and black currants, loganberries, etc. I usually put mine into the freezer and use them later. Brussels sprouts should be provided with stakes if they are likely to be blown about, otherwise the sprouts themselves will not be firm and hard but will "blow" and be loose and open. Lettuces for harvesting during the winter should be sown now in a cool greenhouse — the seedlings may be planted out in the greenhouse border later. If the lawn is looking rather tired, give it a good feed and make sure not to cut it too short.

In the warm weather, cooking and eating outside, at a barbecue, is becoming more and more popular. Fresh herbs, such as rosemary, sage and thyme, picked from the garden and put onto the coals, will add extra scent and flavour to the cooking. However, do watch where you position the barbecue as it gives off a great deal of heat and this could cause scorch marks on plants — also remember to keep small children well away from the fire.

I hate to say it, but you should be thinking about Christmas now and buying in bulbs for indoor flowering. Make sure that you get the prepared bulbs — these are the ones which have had special heat treatment. Narcissi (Paper White), hyacinths (Pink Rosalie), blue ostara and daffodils (Golden Harvest), are excellent for this purpose. You will need bulb fibre, moist peat, a little charcoal (which helps to keep compost sweet), oyster shell and good drainage. Plant in pots and bowls and stand them in a dark place, in the cool, until shoots are about $\frac{3}{4}$ to 1 inch high (it takes about 9–12 weeks). Gradually bring the bulbs into the light, preferably in a cool room and increase the watering as the flowers open.

PASSION FRUIT WINE
(And this does not mean what you are thinking! The Passion
Fruit or Purple Granadilla is of the Passifloraceae)

Ingredients

4lb Passion Fruit
$^1/_2$lb Barley or Wheat
$3^1/_2$lb Sugar
1 gallon Water
Yeast & Nutrient
Pectic Enzyme

Pick the fruits, cut in half, take out red pips and crush the flesh
with your hands. Pour boiling water over fruit. When cold, add
pectic enzyme. Leave for 48 hours. Strain. Warm up juice, add
sugar, stirring to dissolve. Allow liquor to cool, then add yeast.
Pour into fermenting jar, fit air-lock. When wine is clear, rack
and siphon into bottles.

Jam can also be made from Passion Fruit.

September

TUESDAY SEPTEMBER 1 — Not a very bright day to start the month — I went off to the W.I. Home Economics Committee meeting in Ipswich. This is a group which meets four or five times a year to plan special events for Institute members covering such topics as cookery, gardening or preserves. In the afternoon I managed to tidy up my bedrooms. I also needed to move some of the furniture around as I am having a friend to stay for a few days.

I noticed today that the swallows are beginning to congregate on the overhead wires. This is one of the first signs of autumn when they start their preparations to fly off to warmer climes for the winter months.

Wednesday September 2 — Once again it is raining — there seems no let up in this wet weather. I went off to Ipswich and did my "Peggy's Patch" programme, then called in at the *East Anglian Daily Times* to drop in my article for the Woman's page in next weeks issue. Before leaving the town I called to see some friends. On my return I found that some of my wine needed racking, so I decided that this had better be my next job.

In the evening some friends called quite unexpectedly and we had a lovely time just chatting about the old times. I went to bed very late, but it has been a welcome change to sit and talk and not to have the television on, do baking or write letters.

Thursday September 3 — W.I. market today, my word how quickly the weeks pass. How I have managed to get flowers and parsley picked in between the showers this year I will never know, and I certainly feel for women in the towns who stand and queue to buy their produce each week in all kinds of weather.

Allan and Jackie called in — the children laughed and asked me why my car was so dirty, they always think it a great joke that my car is always dirty while their dad's car is always so clean.

We had a coach party this afternoon from the Over 60's Club at Barningham, which is somewhere between Diss and Thetford. The weather was cold and miserable, but these nice old souls made the best of it and cheered up a lot when we served them cups of hot tea with buttered scones.

After they left, I embarked on my first lecture of the Autumn, for the W.I. at Brome and Oakley near Diss in Norfolk. It went quite well, but I had an awful journey home in pouring rain. Another full-stop for the farmers, I thought.

Friday September 4 — A much brighter day and it seems a little warmer. I went to see Eric Overall and Gerald Stiff this morning, both are well-known in the Ipswich area for flower arranging. They had set up some beautiful flower arranging exhibits for me to photograph for my forthcoming trip to America. Eric is very clever; he makes his own containers and is one of the county's professional demonstrators. From there I went on to have my hair cut. After I returned home I did a lot of watering in the greenhouses; it is surprising how a little sun soon warms the greenhouse up and dries out the plants.

This evening I went back to Ipswich for the radio programme and as I drove in I noticed that the corn was still quite green and I'm afraid that much of it will be useless this season, and hardly worth combining.

Saturday September 5 — Got up early and picked a lot of dried flowers, I also cut some more red cabbage and beetroot ready for pickling. I was glad that I made an early start as by ten o'clock it was pouring with rain again. I went to Chelmondiston where I was judging at their Show. Mr. Geoffrey Frost from the village was going as well so he gave me a lift in his car. I was judging the wine, cake and craft classes, and I must say that I thought that their crafts were outstanding. All in all it was a very good Show, it is remarkable what some of these comparatively small villages come up with. We arrived back at Charsfield at about two in the afternoon, and after having a bite to eat I cut up my red cabbage. After tea, I spent the evening sorting out my slides for America, and I was doing this from half past seven through until 12.15 a.m. It's amazing the time it takes to sort out transparencies; it is certainly a job for the winter evenings. I didn't need any rocking to get to sleep I can tell you.

Sunday September 6 — As there was no early service this morning, I did a bit of cooking and tidying up the house. By three o'clock it was raining and continued right through the afternoon and early evening; needless to say it stopped any visitors coming for today, so I sat and did my newspaper articles to cover the time that I spend in the U.S.A. Although I am looking forward to my time abroad it does mean that I have to do six weeks work in advance.

My son, David, 'phoned to say that he is having problems with the purchase of his new house; the price has risen £3000 since he started to buy it, some ten weeks ago, that really is too bad. I asked him whether he was still going on with it as it seemed such a big jump, but as he said if he gave up now, he would be back at square one, and would probably lose money on the deal.

Monday September 7 — A dull start to the day, although it did manage to clear up later. I got a number of letters done early, then went on to blood donors. From there I paid a visit to Notcutts and took more photos of shrubs in readiness for my forthcoming trip to the States. This evening I attended a Parish Council Meeting — nothing exciting happened. The subject of new houses came up, but it always seems so sad that despite the need for housing, so many plans which come in are turned down by the planning authorities simply because they do not quite agree with the green belt regulations.

I also had a sad thing happen today at home. As I went into the chicken run I found six of my chickens had been killed. What had killed them I didn't know, but I suspect that a rat had done it. They had been growing well and had just started to fly up and climb over the wire netting run which I had made for them.

Tuesday September 8 — Had to give the W.I. market a miss today, as I had an appointment at St. John's Church at Woodbridge; a lady wanted to discuss the flowers for her daughter's wedding. I got back home in time to welcome a group of ladies from somewhere near Bury St. Edmunds, they had called in to look at the garden on the way to Southwold. After they left I got my things together ready to make a journey to Stanway near Colchester where I was to give a talk to what turned out to be a large group of ladies.

Wednesday September 9 — This morning I went to Ipswich to do my regular radio programme, and although it was raining early on it did manage to clear up later in the day, but it is still not the weather to attract people to visit gardens. Soon after arriving home I was off again, this time to Aldeburgh where I was to give the ladies of the Women's Institute a talk on my garden. I must say that I enjoy going out to talk and lecture, and I already appear to have a fairly busy season booked. The evenings certainly pull in now, and it is getting dark by half-past seven, so after the watering is done there is very little time left to do anything else outside. This is a busy time now for taking cuttings, and I noticed that some geranium cuttings which I took only three weeks ago are doing quite nicely.

Thursday September 10 — I had some friends call on me early today — Canon Daniel and Deaconess Betty Jones. The Canon used to be the rector here at Charsfield some years ago and it was good to see them again. After they left I went to Kesgrave to see Eric Overall and to talk about the slides which I had taken at his house a few days before, I then went on to give a talk at the Bury St. Edmunds W.I. Back late in the afternoon I set to and made a number of casseroles for the freezer, these will keep Ronnie going when I am away in America — actually the freezer is getting full up with prepared meals!

Friday September 11 — Some people may think I am rather cruel, but today I killed six of my chickens. The problem is that I have so many now, that some just had to go, and another reason is that I did not want to leave too much work for when I am away. I had better not tell my brother that these are going into the casseroles!! This morning I have given the house a good clean through including the windows, and everything is spick and span. The garden is looking pretty still, now that the second flush of roses are coming out, it was such a pity that the rain spoilt the first blooms. Although the blackberries, I notice, are not so good this year, and this is understandable with all the wet weather that we have had, the plums and sloes have been excellent, with trees and bushes full of lovely fruit. Many of the hedgerows are covered with berries as well.

Saturday September 12 — I had the chimney swept this morning, so I was about early. After I had cleared up I went and arranged the flowers in St. Peter's church in the village — it was my turn this week.

It makes a change to be at home on a Saturday, no judging today. I did a lot of hardwood pruning and took quite a number of cuttings. I was able to tidy up the greenhouse, and removed some of the old tomato plants so that I was able to put the shelf back.

Sunday September 13 — A nice day for a change — we had the garden open for the Hungerford Appeal. The weather kept fine and we had a lot of visitors throughout the day. My friend Sheila came to help me and about £100 was raised. We were kept busy for most of the day, as I sold cups of tea, scones and buns. In the evening some friends called round and I showed them some of my slides. It really is a delight to look at some of the old pictures, and to see some of the changes which have taken place since I actually took the photos.

Monday September 14 — Finished my garden notes off, then did some summer pruning of shrubs which had finished flowering. I finished boiling up my Christmas puddings, then, in the afternoon went over to the Old Peoples Club at Combs, near Stowmarket, to judge their small Show and give them a talk about my garden. This evening I went to Bramford Women's Institute to show slides on the countryside. On the whole this has seemed to be a busy day, and I was glad to get into my bed tonight.

Tuesday September 15 — Another bonus it seems, with a nice warm day. I got an early start and made Runner Bean Chutney, I also made a Christmas cake and eight pounds of plum jam; my sitting room is beginning to look like a shop with all my jars of pickles and jams. I shall have to get it all put away in my cupboard upstairs; people often laugh at me when I say that I am going to the bedroom to get a jar of jam, but the cupboard up there is a dark and fairly large one and I am able to store a lot in it.

Mrs. Parkinson, a friend of mine called to gather some flowers, as she was going to give a church flower demonstration.

Wednesday September 16 — I didn't think the fine weather could last; it was raining again early this morning. I went to Ipswich and did my "Peggy's Patch" programme, then went on to the Cash and Carry to restock my larder, as well as buying some bulbs—hyacinths and narcissi. I know I am late in planting them this year, but if I don't get flowers for Christmas, at least I shall have the pleasure of seeing them in the new year. I notice that the song of the robin has changed to its autumn tune now, and I still see the swallows lined up on the telephone wires — I expect they will be off any day now. Today, I picked asparagus peas, they made a lovely change, though a bit late in the season. You do need quite a lot even for one serving, so they are not an ideal crop to grow for hungry families.

Thursday September 17 — I went to the W.I. market then did some shopping in Woodbridge where I found a nice pair of leather sandals in a sale, for £7 — this made up for the pair I lost. I called and had lunch with Jackie and the children, then went up to the florists in Woodbridge and picked up flowers, for another wedding. Having collected what I wanted I came straight home and put them in some deep containers in the church. Later in the day I developed such a bad head that I had to cancel a talk in Ipswich. This is something I hate to do, but there was no way I could have coped with it tonight. During the day I had a 'phone call from the travel agent to say that there was a change of flights on the day I go to America. What with this and the very sultry weather today, there is little wonder that my head aches.

Friday September 18 — Very busy today — I went first to St. Peter's church and decorated it with flowers for the wedding, then came home and had a quick bath before going off to the Old Peoples Department at Heath Road Hospital in Ipswich where I was to open the Harvest Festival. I was then picked up by Mike Richards who drove me to Bury St. Edmunds, as we were going to do a live broadcast of the Gardening Hour to celebrate "Bury In Bloom". I got home at ten o'clock feeling I'd had enough.

Saturday September 19 — Another busy day. I went and opened the Heart Foundation Autumn Fair at the Cornhill in Ipswich at half-past nine this morning, then went on to judge flowers at Grundisburgh at 10.45. This was followed by another appointment at mid-day, this time at British Telecom at Martlesham where I was to judge craft and cookery exhibits. The crafts were outstanding, and I had a real job to pick the winners, they were all so very good. It was absolutely pouring with rain when I got home at about 3 pm. I changed my clothes, then sat down and pickled my onions as some had started to go bad, because of all the wet weather. I also made twelve pounds of crab apple jelly — this turned out well and is a lovely colour.

Sunday September 20 — I woke up feeling tired today and would have been quite happy to have spent an extra hour or two in bed! But a "job-list" started to form in my mind so I was soon on the move. After a quick "clean-up" after breakfast, I started to organise the various items I shall need on my American trip, then got down to completing six weekly articles for the *East Anglian Daily Times* to cover the period I shall be away. I also sorted out some of my slides during the evening, trying to make up my mind which to use over there. Ron and I also sampled some of my 1986 Apple wine, which is quite good.

Monday September 21 — For my first task today I wrote a few letters, then once more I started to sort out slides — it is surprising how long it takes to select those which will be most effective. I tidied up the house then went to Melton to look after Russell and Sarah. We walked up to Woodbridge town to do some shopping. They are good children, and never ask me to buy them things, although they are very interested in all they see, and ask me to tell them about the various items in the shop windows.

After tea I went over to the hedge in my neighbours orchard and picked twenty two pounds of blue plums. I wish I knew a bit more of the history of this hedge — this might give me a clue as to the variety. They are rather like a sloe although slightly larger; I wonder whether they could be a black bullace or even a damson, but never mind, whatever they are they make delicious wine. Later in the evening Ron helped me prick some, which I put into gin ready for a Christmas drink, and the rest I made into wine.

I was sad to-day to hear that a dear friend has been taken into hospital at Addenbrooks in Cambridge, with Wilson's Disease. Deborah is a lovely girl, only 23 years old, she is a florist by profession, and has helped me so often with flowers for weddings.

Tuesday September 22 — Another letter arrived today from the U.S.A. They need more photographs for the Press, so off I went early, to post these. On the way dropped some blue plums — or sloes — in at my friend Claude's at Wickham Market. After I arrived home, Marion, another friend called, and we had lunch together. I have known Marion for a long time. She used to live over at Shrubbery Farm as a small child, and my late husband worked there for her parents — Mr. & Mrs. Pudney. Sadly Marion lost her husband with a crippling disease, about a year ago. She brought me some crab apples, and I think I will use these for making into wine.

Mr. Clarke from Notcutts came during the day. He brought a forklift truck and a photographer to take photos of the garden. He felt it would be a good idea to get pictures taken from a height so that the Americans could see just how much I could cram into a small garden. In the evening I made my way to Maldon in Essex to give a talk to members of a Garden Society, it was rather a long way there — over fifty-two miles, so Sheila came with me as company.

Wednesday September 23 — A lovely bright and warm day. I went and picked up some of my dresses which had been at the dressmakers for alterations, then I went on to do my programme. Leaving Ipswich, I drove over to see Beth Chatto and her famous garden at Elmstead Market near Colchester. She had promised me some slides for my forthcoming trip, some particular flower pictures that I had asked her for. We had a good chat about the trip, and about many gardening matters, and I eventually arrived home at about three o'clock. After a cup of tea I picked some swiss chard ready for the market tomorrow, then made some plum jam. During the evening I had a 'phone call from my son David to tell me that Deborah was very ill and was going to have a liver transplant early tomorrow morning. Poor girl, I pray that she pulls through.

Thursday September 24 — I went to the W.I. market, taking various items, including a lot of my Bramley apples, as I have so many this year. I then went on to have my hair set, before calling in to see the family at Melton and having coffee with them. Then, back to Woodbridge where I collected more flowers for a wedding, before coming home to Charsfield where I cleared the church of last week's wedding flowers. This evening I had a meeting here at the house with some ladies from the village to arrange the Charsfield Over 60's Christmas Party.

Friday September 25 — Another bright day, which still feels like a bonus after the wretched summer we have had. But, there is a nip in the air, and it begins to feel a bit like autumn. I went off to St. John's church at Woodbridge to arrange flowers for a wedding, this is one which Deborah should have done, but because she was so ill had asked me if I could help out.

I got home late in the afternoon and managed to move my glass cloches on to seedlings of spring cabbage, for they didn't seem to be growing very well. I then got my notes together and went off to do the gardening programme.

The farmers are very busy at the moment, trying to get the remainder of the corn in. The women are picking apples — Cox's and Bramleys up at the Hall, this is the large fruit farm in the village. It seems early to be picking, but they are then taken off to the cold store so it doesn't seem to matter.

Saturday September 26 — A cold nip in the air again this morning, and I wouldn't be surprised if there was a little frost. I went to Laxfield to judge the floral exhibits at their show, it was a small Show, but the standard was very high. I arrived back in good time to get lunch then I sorted out cheese and wine for the Disabled Group Social Evening which is held in the village hall. It turned out to be a very enjoyable evening, and all the drink we had was home-made wine — altogether we made £100 during the evening. Claude and Iris came over to help, with Ronnie, and at the close we all ended up here for coffee, so I didn't get to bed until half-past one — in the morning.

Sunday September 27 — Not so many people around today. There was only £10 in the box, however the garden still looks very pretty. In between attending to visitors I wrote up some notes, and also had a go at sorting out the papers on my desk.

Monday September 28 — Made some red tomato chutney, also sorted out jam jars this morning — this seems to be a big problem nowadays, trying to find one pound jars; there are so many sizes and shapes but the W.I. market do like their produce to be in 1lb jars if possible.

I heard today that poor Debbie was not so good, she has been through an awful time I think, and although I racked my sloe and crab apple wine and put it into one gallon jars, my mind was only half on the job.

David rang me from Bermuda, he and Norine are there on holiday. They have had a hurricane and he said that the storm had been very bad indeed but that they were safe although they had moved to another part of the island where they could get drinking water. It is rather odd that I shall be flying out to America as they are flying home!

Tuesday September 29 — As my air tickets were at Ipswich, I went and picked them up this morning. Sheila came with me as, at one o'clock, I was to be a guest and give a talk to the St. John and Red Cross Librarians Association luncheon at Grundisburgh village hall. It was all very pleasant and I met Lady Rowley, who is the Association President. I arrived home at 4.30 pm and then rushed round to the surgery to collect some pills which I will need when I am in the States. I spent the evening making some apple and ginger jam.

Wednesday September 30 — I took Ronnie with me this morning to Ipswich to visit our brother Peter and his wife, May, for the day. It makes a change for him to have a day off but unfortunately, I had to get home early to meet my visitors from a Harris's coach party which came during the afternoon. It has been one of those days where I didn't seem to stop at all, what with the visitors and also trying to get my produce ready for the W.I. market; this will be the last one I shall help with, until after my American lecture tour. Iris and Claude brought Ronnie home from Wickham Market during the evening and I finished checking my slides.

The weather has been rather nice this week; it does make a wonderful difference to life, to be sure.

I suppose September will be remembered by the farmers in East Anglia because of the crippling sugar beet disease, rhizomania, which struck at a farm near Bury St. Edmunds.

There were also angry scenes this month at Ipswich County Hall, as Suffolk Education Chiefs decided to close schools in Reydon, Wrentham and Henham.

HINTS FOR SEPTEMBER

For people taking a late holiday and are a bit worried about their house plants, try this hint. Place the pots in the sink, on an old piece of cloth and stand a bucket of water on the draining board. Take lengths of thick knitting wool, putting one end in the bucket and the other end on the plant and this will act as a capillary filler.

Maincrop potatoes should be lifted now — after digging them up, leave them to dry for a few hours in the sun before placing them in sacks or strong paper bags and store in a frost free place. Don't use plastic bags, as the potatoes will 'sweat'. Harvest onions by placing them in the sunshine to dry completely and rub off the old skins before storing in a cool dry shed.

Take the opportunity of giving the glasshouse a good clean out and wash down once the tomatoes have finished. Put up some polythene at the end of the month as this help to conserve heat and reduce the heating bills. We have another old saying "what July and August do not boil, September cannot fry" and indeed, by this time, high summer temperatures are usually a thing of the past.

September tasks include removing summer bedding plants and getting the ground ready for spring replacements. Lawns will need a deal of attention, the bulb planting season is here and there is a general need to cut down old plants and tidy up — remember that the evenings will be getting shorter and cooler so cuttings will take longer to root. If you have seen a plant doing well in the baskets or containers, take cuttings early in the month. This is the time to plant evergreens but make sure that you have a good ball of soil round the roots. If we get a dry time, spraying the foliage with soft water will help the plant. House plants should be brought inside, making sure that no slugs are clinging round the pots. Reduce watering and feeding, especially the cacti and succulents.

Pick all tomatoes which have been grown outside as they are unlikely to ripen any more. Green tomatoes can be made into a delicious chutney, and to ripen green tomatoes, place them on old egg trays together with one red tomato, and put into a box — you will soon find that they have turned red.

Autumn leaves can be a nuisance so keep them raked up regularly. If you have a garden pond, scoop them off the water. Spreading plastic netting over the pool may help to keep it free of leaves.

Villages hold their Harvest Festivals during this month and it is nice to see the church windows decked out with produce from one's own garden, all kinds of flowers and foliage being used for this purpose, as well as eggs, fruit and many kinds of vegetables and often a huge marrow with the name of the village church inscribed on it. This is done by scratching the letters on the young marrow and, as it grows, so does the name — young children especially love to do this and watch it grow.

CRUNCHY BLACKBERRY FLAN

Ingredients

6oz Digestive biscuits
2oz butter
3 cooking apples
5oz brown sugar
1 large teacup of blackberries
1 large teacup custard, yoghurt or cream
1 tablespoon white sugar

Crush the biscuits with a rolling pin and put them in a saucepan
with butter and stir, heating these together. Turn out the crumb
mixture into a glass dish. Peel and core the apples; using no water,
simmer until tender. Add 2oz brown sugar and stir until they are
soft. In another pan, put the blackberries with the tablespoon of
sugar and stir over a gentle heat until they are soft. Place the apple
mixture on the crunchy base and over the apple spread the thick
custard, yoghurt or cream. Spread the blackberries on to the
custard, yoghurt or cream and cover with the remaining brown
sugar. The whole dish can then be placed under the grill to brown
the sugar.
    This is delicious hot or cold.

October

THURSDAY OCTOBER 1 — I took some onions, swiss chard and Bramley apples to the W.I. market. After the market finished, I returned to find that my car would not start so I had to call out my local garage engineer to have a look at it. Fortunately, it turned out to be a fault with the battery terminals and eventually I did get home. As Ron was on holiday, I got lunch ready for both of us then I went along to decorate the church window for the Harvest Festival. It seemed rather sad to be pulling up all the vegetables and picking flowers from the garden just now; there is a hint of Autumn in the air. I also managed to move plants into the greenhouse as a precaution against a frost — I have a lot of tender plants still outside.

Friday October 2 — Woke up with an awful headache today — I certainly didn't need this with all my last minute jobs to do. I went to see a chiropodist today as I need to have my feet in good working order for all the walking I shall be doing during the next few weeks. I then helped Ron to pack all the garden tables and chairs in the top shed for the winter months. I made three more cottage pies — my freezer is absolutely full to the top with food now but, at least, I shall know that Ronnie will have a meal each day, ready cooked; all he will have to do is to pop his choice into the microwave, and there are also plenty of cakes for any visitors he may have.

I went and did my last gardening programme for four weeks,

then came home and finished putting the remainder of my preserves away in the cupboard upstairs. These have been standing all over the sitting-room floor —jars of jam and pickles everywhere.

Saturday October 3 — A nice day but I was so busy, I didn't seem to stop, only for a bite to eat. There are so many last minute jobs to do before I leave tomorrow. Ron started to cut some of my fuchsias down, these we packed under the benches in the greenhouse. I also finished cleaning the house right through. It was late in the evening before I managed to finish packing my suitcases, then I had a bath and got into bed just after 1.00 am.

Sunday October 4 — My son Allan picked me up from my home at 11 am to drive me to Gatwick Airport. Jackie, Russell and Sarah came too, but we dropped them off to visit her parents at Brentwood. It was one o'clock before we reached the airport, I never realised how far it was out of London. What a lot of people, all going out of, or coming into, the country. I went and checked in with Virgin Airlines and could hardly believe the size of the plane on which I would be flying, together with four hundred other passengers. My seat was situated near the window — what an experience!! Sitting and looking out over England far below, it did not seem as if we were travelling so fast. Soon the air hostess came round and gave out headphones (these could be hired to watch the film shows). Drinks were then served — I had a whisky and ginger as, I must admit, my tummy was rather "jumpy". In the meantime, the captain told us to put our watches back from 5.30 pm to 12.30 pm, so we immediately gained five hours. The air hostess then served a hot meal of steak, chicken or fish, with vegetables and afterwards a sweet and also coffee — all very enjoyable. The only thing I could fault was that there was not enough room to stretch my legs and I soon got cramp.

Afternoon tea of scones, cream, jam and cakes and plenty to drink, was served about four hours later. A film was being shown, but I passed the time by looking out of the window at the lovely colours of the sky, the reds and blues. As the plane reached America, I noticed some snow and one of the other passengers told me that it was in the city of Albany (a freak snowstorm — unheard of at this time of the year). We could see the Hudson River and the captain explained that a lot of aeroplanes followed the course of the river on the flight into New York airport. I landed at Newark, New Jersey and had to wait for one and a half hours before catching the next plane to Syracuse. I was feeling rather lost but people were very kind and soon showed me which way to go. I then boarded the next plane, a much smaller one this time, only one hundred passengers altogether, for the three-quarters of an hour journey.

I was met at the airport by Patsy Hovenden, the lady who had made this trip possible. We loaded my cases into her large Buick car and drove another fifty miles to her home in Utica. I got into bed at 1.30 am, feeling excited but quite shattered!!

Monday October 5 — Woke up to find the sun streaming in through my bedroom window, it was 7.00 am U.S. time. The view was beautiful, with trees in colours of red, orange and gold — there was the Mohawk Valley which could be seen from the back of the house. We had breakfast, then Patsy took me to Dodgeville where we met Carol Gate, who lives in a lovely house which has a small lodge used as a gift shop where dried flowers, herbs and a wide variety of souvenirs, are sold. They even have a spiral staircase lined with cards and gifts. The top floor is called "Gate House Herbs" and I can smell this little shop, even as I write this. Cheese and herb sandwiches were offered, also a delicious sweet cake with rum and ice-cream, and coffee with an unusual flavour of orange and chocolate, all very scrumptious.

Carol's house was one of the old American-style buildings containing a lot of wood and dark interior panels and she told me that she was the third generation of her family to live there. Set in five acres of woodland, it certainly is a charming place.

Our next stop was Lyndon Lyon Nurseries, where the first Double Pink African Violet was raised, so you can guess that there are greenhouses full of these plants, with flowers of every description. I asked the nurseryman if he had ever met one of my friends, Tony Clements, a well-known English grower and he told me that he had supplied Tony with plants — it is indeed a small world. As I left the nursery, I spotted a blue jay, this was about the same size as our native variety but a very pretty blue.

The next places we visited were Jordanville and Herkimer, passing a Russian monastery on the way. Patsy tells me that a lot of Russians, including Rostropovitch, the world famous conductor and cellist who has made many concert appearances at the annual Aldeburgh Festival, just up the road from Charsfield, live in this part of the country. On then to Mohawk Valley, the view and colours of the trees were simply wonderful — rather like Scotland, I thought, with the mountains except that they don't have such dazzling colours there.

Patsy then drove on to Cooperstown where we called in at a cider mill called Fly Creek Mill. I saw some fine displays of pumpkins all ready for All Hallows Day (31st October), something we don't seem to do in England. We stopped at an ice-cream shop and I had my first taste of American ice-cream then we sat by the side of Otsego Lake which, I am told, is nine miles long and one mile wide and is an excellent place for fishing and swimming. We arrived back at Patsy's home at half-past six, after a really lovely warm day out, together with one roll of film ready for the developer.

Tuesday October 6 — I had a splitting headache when I woke this morning at about five o'clock, but after taking two tablets and opening the bedroom window, this soon disappeared — I am so used to sleeping with my windows open at home, both in summer and winter. The first thing I did was to write up my diary, then I rang Lindsay Bond-Totten who is the Director of Pittsburgh Civic Garden Center, just to let her know that I had arrived.

After breakfast, I helped Patsy to cut the lawn. Her house is up for sale and Tony, her husband, who is a doctor, has moved to a hospital in Washington D.C. to work, so she will be leaving there soon. She is going to miss this lovely detached graystone house, with its one and a half acres. I thought it a strange custom that the house agent has the key to your property and when he is bringing a client to look around, he simply phones up and you then clear out of the house. I would have thought that it would have been better to have been there yourself, if only to answer any questions about the property.

Later that day I was asked to do a flower arrangement in the Utica Grace Church, so that the local *Observer Dispatch* newspaper reporter could come along and do an interview with me; this was to give advance publicity for Utica, who were first fund-raisers of Hospice Auxiliary. I did a large pedestal arrangement of orange gladioli, yellow and white chrysanthemums with green foliage. After we left the church, I was taken to meet Susan Kiesel, of Cotton Wood Cottage, Saquoit. The journey involved a nice ride into typical countryside with small farms. As we went along, I noticed so much of the blue Michaelmas Daisy and Golden Rod growing by the roadside, a haze of blue and gold everywhere and, of course, the general effect is so different from England, as there is so much space between cottages and houses. Susan's house was real American and she had just opened a little wooden craft shop, with lots of dried flowers, wreaths, cards and candles for sale. A big thing over there is that nearly everyone has a wreath or pretty hat hung on their door; they are very decorative. We then went to have supper with Sue and Tony Horvath in their lovely home, where I had steak followed by raspberry tart (very good). Feeling very tired, I finally got into bed at 11.30 pm.

Wednesday October 7 — Heavy rain woke me up at four o'clock and I got up at 6.30 and did some reading. I made Patsy some scones, which were for the Hospice tea the next day, also dug up and re-potted some shrubs ready for when she moves to her new home. After lunch, we went shopping in a mall, rather like a huge shopping centre under cover, in which you can buy anything, from food to furniture. I saw my first Christmas tree, gaily decorated and I also took a photo of a display of muffins and doughnuts, some thirty varieties. By the way, I had a muffin for breakfast, they are rather filling — I would say, like eating a fruit bun which we serve with our teas. Patsy took me to a garden centre but it was not very good, a very poor selection of plants and inferior specimens at that. We left to drive home as Patsy had arranged a dinner party in my honour and had invited the entire committee of Hospice helpers to meet me. She cooked a tasty beef and pepper dish, with rice and I helped to make a spinach salad. For a sweet, we had orange cake and raspberry pavlova. During the evening, I was given presents of wreaths and trays, by the Hospice committee. Another enjoyable but somewhat tiring day.

Thursday October 8 — Raining today!! I am just getting over the time difference and am not feeling quite so tired. I went to the hairdresser at 7.30 am, a very nice lady called Mary Lou did my hair. When it came to paying, she refused to take any money but asked me to put it towards the Hospice fund, which I did gladly. At ten o'clock, I was taken to meet the staff at the Hospice and I was able to give them a little talk on how we raise money in England for our local hospice — I told them about my garden and also the other forms of fund raising that we employ. At mid-day, Patsy took me to the Suny College of Technology in Marcy, Utica, where I was to give my first talk in America. Each garden club involved had decorated a little corner with flowers, etc., to welcome me on my visit. The lecture started at 1.30 pm with about two hundred people in the hall and before I went on stage, the local TV were there to do an interview.

After I had finished my talk, an English tea of fruit cake, shortbread and scones was served — I think however, I shall have to go back to show the ladies how to make an English scone as I have never seen such shapes before in all my life!

A cutting from a newspaper and a photo of me doing the flowers in Utica Grace Church was sent in, together with a cheque for one thousand dollars, by a grateful gentleman, so the

Hospice committee was very pleased and as a token of appreciation, I was given a very pretty corsage and also a book about herbs.

Patsy had a friend to stay the night, an Irish girl called Jill, whose home was in County Cork and we had a very interesting chat over supper. Patsy had been given tickets for a concert by the Utica Symphony Orchestra, which we attended. Charles Kuralt, a well-known TV personality read a Lincoln Portrait and the music included works by Beethoven and Bartok, which was very enjoyable. The theatre was one of the prettiest I have seen, with lots of traditional gold and plush, but like all old theatres, it needs a lot of money to be spent on it. On leaving the concert, we walked across the road for drinks and "nibbles" to eat. I met many people there who had been to my lecture and who said how much they had enjoyed it. The weather has been very cold today. I finally got into bed at 12.00 am, tired, but having had another memorable day.

Friday October 9 — Patsy cooked me blueberry pancakes for breakfast. The weather this morning was bright and sunny but with very cold winds. I was collected at ten o'clock by Mary Wilcox, secretary of the Hospice Auxiliary, who took me first to the television station, where I was presented with a video of the programme which I had been on, yesterday. She then took me sight-seeing and afterwards we went to meet ten of the Hospice staff for lunch at Clinton House Restaurant, Clinton. I had crab salad, followed by chocolate fudge ice-cream — boy! was I fulfilled when I left that restaurant! Jo Horvath drove me back, a very pleasant ride, past Hamilton University, arriving at Patsy's home at about five o'clock. I then helped her to pack, as she was leaving her home for four weeks. I wrote some cards and, after a light supper, decided to have an early night.

Saturday October 10 — We were up early this morning and took Patsy's two cats to "The Cats Meow", a cats' home, then loaded the car with boxes and cases ready to make our way to Niagara. We left Utica at twelve o'clock and went on the thruway, which is rather like our motorway — in some states you have to pay to go on them. If you break down, you hang a white handkerchief out of the window and a patrolling policeman will soon come along to help you. We made tracks for Buffalo, going past Lake Ontario and travelling west to Finger Lake region. Our stop for lunch, a picnic, was a short one, as the winds were very cold. I watched two men in the picnic area going through the rubbish bins and taking out all the old beer cans and bottles — Patsy told me that this is how some people make a living, as there was five cents given on the "empties".

Our next stop was Sonnenberg Gardens, a pleasant place with old gardens and greenhouses. It is in the city of Canandaigua, just a few minutes drive north of Canandaigua Lake, in the heart of New York Finger Lakes. The forty-room mansion was a fine place to visit and according to the guide, the late-Victorian garden was one of the most magnificent ever created in America. I would have liked to stop much longer and to have been able to walk through the Japanese and Italian sections. There was even a wine-tasting room (which we did sample!). We then made our way to Buffalo on the outskirts of Niagara; we got a bit lost but finally arrived at 7.00 pm, after travelling some three hundred miles. Your eyes have to be everywhere looking for road signs after crossing Peace Bridge, between Canada and the United States. We had quite a job to find rooms for the night, as so many places were full. We walked around for a while, then had a meal in a restaurant which overlooks the Falls. I just can't describe the noise of the water cascading down — it was pouring with rain but so many people were out sight-seeing, even in the dark and no one was worrying about the weather. There are coloured lights which are switched on at night and these shine out over the water — pink, green, blue — it really is a spectacular sight. We went back to our rooms, tired but excited, and soon fell asleep.

Sunday October 11 — We were up early again this morning and were walking around the falls by ten o'clock. We spent one and a half to two hours, just walking and looking — the rain had stopped and it was a sight I shall never forget, well worth coming all these miles to see. At the Horseshoe Falls, the water is falling down about one hundred and seventy feet. We did not go on the boat trip on the "Maid of the Mist", but instead went down 125 feet by elevator, to the look-out platforms and then walked another six hundred and fifty feet to view the falls — yellow raincoats and hats were provided. We walked back to the car through the parks and gardens, where I saw a statue of King George VI — dear old England, I thought. The gardens were some of the best I had seen so far, lovely beds of Busy Lizzies, Lantanas, Cannas and Ferns; they had not suffered a frost yet. Patsy took me for a brunch, as we had not had anything to eat since the previous night. We called in at the Niagara Golf Club and I had asparagus pancake, bacon, potato and sliced fruit, all on one plate — it was all very tasty indeed.

As we left Niagara, we passed the School of Horticulture, which is world-famous, being the only residential school for apprentice gardeners in Canada. Visitors can stroll around the campus and view the garden display area at their leisure free of charge. We then stopped to look at the floral clock which is some forty feet in diameter and planted with 15,000 plants, a new design being used for each face each year.

We went on again at twelve o'clock, towards Pittsburgh. One thing I did notice, the motorways were so clean — no litter about anywhere. There were also fields and fields of grape-vines. Still driving south-west, I saw Lake Erie, one of the Great Lakes of America, and we then came into the state of Pennsylvania. One sign I noticed read "bridges may be icy", so you can guess what the weather is like there, in the winter.

We arrived at the home of two more of Patsy's English friends, Diana and Ernie Siddons. Ernie is an accountant and they moved from England about ten years ago — they have a lovely home, standing in an acre of woodland. Once again, I had an enjoyable meal, this time of steak and salad, after which we all went to the Carnegie Music Hall in Pittsburgh, to see "A Gershwin Gala". This was a lovely musical treat and the musicians included a

choir of seventy voices. We got back at 11.45 pm and were soon
fast asleep in bed.

Monday October 12 — The time seems to fly by so quickly, but
I do miss my *East Anglian* (daily paper) at breakfast time! It's
strange not getting news from England; even the television has
very little British news. I was up at half-past six, then sat and
wrote cards to my friends at home.

Today is Columbus Day, so a holiday for the postman and some
other working people. I was taken to down-town Pittsburgh to
see the views, then to Mount Washington by the Monongahela
Incline. This is a funicular — cable railway. The view overlook-
ing Pittsburgh was wonderful, featuring so many bridges. We
then went to see some of the buildings. The one which stood out
for me, was the Pittsburgh Plate-Glass building, the architecture
being partly like our modern churches and it also made me think
of Willis Faber in Ipswich, one of the most admired glass-faced
buildings in Europe.

Patsy then took me to the back streets, to a fish restaurant,
which had every kind of fish you could think of, but you had to
stand to eat. It is fashionable for workers to come and have fish-
roll or hot fish soup, but not fish'n'chips! I had a cup of sea food
chowder and it was very good.

We then made our way to visit the Pittsburgh Garden Center,
to make arrangements for my talk there the next day. I met
Lindsay Bond-Totten — Director of P.C.G.C. (so nice to meet
her after months of correspondence and telephone calls), who
made me very welcome and put me at ease. We then left to meet
a reporter who was going to do some articles in the local
newspaper, about my visit to the U.S.A. After we had supper,
Diana had invited friends, including some English ladies who
were coming to my lecture, for desserts. This form of entertaining
is a new thing to me but it is quite popular here. Once again, I had
no trouble getting to sleep, after another crowded day.

Tuesday October 13 — Another nice day — bright and sunny.

I was taken to the Garden Center for my talk, which was at 10.30 and my first lecture was about growing flowers and shrubs for the flower-arranger. We then stopped for lunch and everyone was given a small paper bag containing sandwiches of tuna, ham and cheese, a carton of salad, a cookie and an apple, after which coffee was served.

I then gave my next lecture, the subject being "What to look for on the showbench — varieties of vegetables and flowers, wine and cookery". Many of the ladies who seemed to enjoy my talk, stayed behind to chat with me.

Following this, Lindsay took me to visit the Fipps Garden and Greenhouses, down town and we got back to Diana's at half-past five. I then changed, had a quick shower, and was taken to have supper with Ann Munson, another English lady — stuffed fish and pecan pie were served and were most appetising. Into bed at 10.30 pm at the end of a most enjoyable day.

Wednesday October 14 — Sharp frost, white everywhere! Woke up with one of my bad heads — the Americans do keep their houses much warmer than we do and I can't stand warm bedrooms, or windows sealed up, even in winter.

I was taken to King's Restaurant for breakfast, and to say farewell to the eight ladies, whom I met, from Pittsburgh. When we arrived, at 8.15 am, it was full of people eating, for example, two eggs, two sausages, melon, fried bread and potatoes, all on one plate. And who can eat blueberry pancakes so early in the day?

I also said goodbye to Patsy, who has been so kind to me — indeed, had it not been for her, I should never have visited this wonderful country.

A young garden designer then drove me to Dawes Arboretum in Ohio — the journey took three hours and we travelled in brilliant sunshine. I soon began to feel my old self again, after the headache had cleared. The scenery was breathtaking, the maple trees of red and gold looking at their best. I was warmly welcomed by the Director of Horticulture, John Paul Bowes, and his staff, one of whom took me out to lunch and afterwards I was shown around the arboretum. It was a wonderful place — 1,149 acres of woods, meadows, farmland, lakes and gardens. Benjamin Gates Dawes and his wife founded the Arboretum in 1929, to demonstrate the value of various kinds of trees, shrubs and other plants for horticultural research, the culture of trees and shrubs tolerant of Ohio's climate and to increase the overall knowledge of these subjects. The Arboretum is not run for profit, but is a foundation privately operated by a Board of Trustees and financially supported by income from an endowment, from programme sales and donations from the "Friends of Daweswood". It receives no funding from tax revenue or the local state. The grounds are open, free of charge, from dawn till dusk every day except Thanksgiving, Christmas and New Year's Day. There is an attractive visitors' centre open from eight in the morning until five o'clock in the evening, which includes a Gift Center. This garden centre, like a lot more in America, has specialised programmes of study, with certificates offered for Bonsai Botany, Fresh Flower Arranging, Plant Identification, Pruning, Landscaping Design and many others.

The Daweswood Museum is a country-looking American house which they call the Dawes Museum and it is open to the public for tours each day. I had the honour of sleeping there for one night, in a great wooden bed (looking at me, they may have thought that I was a museum piece!). After a quick wash, I was taken to supper by Tammy and Luke, who are on the staff at the Arboretum, at a restaurant in a nearby village. We got back, with fifteen minutes to spare, before I gave my lecture on "My Country Garden", which went down very well. A lady from Newmarket, Mary Wilson, came to have a chat, and I also met a gentleman who was stationed at Woodbridge in 1940, with the 8th Army Air Force.

After the lecture, I was taken by John and his staff, to a cafe-come-pub for drinks, then back to the museum where I took a bath in one of the biggest baths I have ever seen, it was enormous! Afterwards, I soon fell asleep in my large wooden bed. The next day, I was told that the museum was supposed to be haunted but I was so tired, it would have made no difference.

I had to be up before 6.30 am as I was being collected at seven to get to the venue for my next lecture. From the Dawes Arboretum, I especially remember the Blackwall Nut Tree with the nuts lying everywhere; the Staghorn Sumac (Rhus Typhina) with its rich orange and purple colours, some specimens reaching heights of fifteen feet or more (I have also seen these shrubs growing along the wide roads); the Japanese garden; the Prairie paths and the woodlands for which Dawes is famous; I would like to have lingered there much longer

Thursday October 15 — Another sharp frost this morning. Two elderly gentlemen (volunteers of Daweswood who give up their time to work at the Arboretum and show people around) picked me up to travel to Cincinnati. It was a three-hour journey but we stopped on the way to visit one of the well-known Bob Evans restaurants. Here I had some ham and although it was just 8.15 am, the restaurant was very busy. We arrived at Cincinnati Garden Center, where I was taken out to lunch by Ruth, who was the Director. We then went to the Museum and I gave my "Cottage Garden" talk to a large crowd of ladies and gentlemen, after which an English tea was served. I was then taken home by Dorothy Lawton and her husband, with whom I was to spend the evening. I had met Dorothy and her husband earlier in the year, when they had paid a visit to my garden with her sister who lives in Woodbridge. After having a shower and washing my hair, Dorothy kindly set my hair in rollers. We had a very nice supper and then went down town, as Cincinnati was all lit up for the photographers. This is an annual event and there were hundreds of amateurs and professionals taking pictures from all angles — I have never seen a sight like it. There were trucks with their headlights on, which came in for the occasion, all the buildings were lit up, the ferry boats were decked out with all manner of lights and even searchlights helped to light up the night sky. These made me think of the war years when my brother Ron and

I would stand in our garden and watch the American planes going out from the nearby bases, to drop their bombs on Germany. In fact, I went to bed that night and dreamed of the planes going over our house in those wartime years.

Friday October 16 — Left Cincinnati at 8.30 am to go to Mansfield, Ohio — another three-hour drive, and arrived at twelve o'clock to be met by the Director, Ruth Pardue, a charming lady, and her staff who gave me a warm welcome. Her first question was to ask if I had heard about the dreadful storms in England and then to say how sorry she was. You can imagine how I felt, and I tried unsuccessfully to telephone home, but was told that no calls could be made due to storm damage. I gave my talk at 1.00 pm on "Growing Flowers and Shrubs for the Flower Arranger" but my mind was on England and my garden, and wondering if everything was still standing. At the end of the lecture, English tea was served and once again I tried to 'phone home, but still no calls to England.

When I finally managed to get a call through to my brother Ronnie, he told me that my home and greenhouses were safe but the garden fence had blown down. He also said how lucky I had been as the winds had reached hurricane force, the worst for some three hundred years and so much damage had been done around the countryside. There was a lump in my throat and I stood and said a prayer.

One of Ruth's staff took me round the Inniswood Garden Center — this lovely thirty-seven acre estate was left by the late Misses Grace and Mary Innis; Grace loved horticulture and Mary was very interested in ornithology. In 1972, through Grace Innis' generosity on her own behalf and in memory of her sister, Mary, their estate became the nucleus of a 91-acre Metropolitan Park District facility. The home of the late Grace and Mary Innis has been renovated to accommodate public groups — the reception room with cloakroom is a registration area; the multi-purpose room can seat one hundred persons for lectures and there is also a dining-room and kitchen etc. The Innis House has an eight hundred volume reference library.

Ruth took me home as I was to stay with her and her husband for the night — she lives in a nice area of Columbus. She switched on the television to see if there were any pictures of the storm in England and a lady from England said that it was like the war again, with parts of buildings falling down and many trees, especially in Kew Gardens, which was devastated — this made me feel very sad. Ruth, her husband and I, went for a meal at the "Peppercorn Duck", a very exclusive hotel. I had cream seafood soup, a whole lobster and salad. I have never seen such a fine variety of salads. For sweet, there was a super chocolate dessert and I finished with strawberries and melons dipped in chocolate, plus some wine. I thought to myself "My God, you must have put on so much weight with these calories tonight", but it's a meal I shall never forget. We then drove home, seeing the highlights of the city of Columbus and went to bed at 10.45 pm.

Saturday October 17 — After an early breakfast, Ruth drove me to her garden centre, where I was due to give a talk at ten o'clock. A buffet lunch was laid on and afterwards I answered questions and chatted to some of the volunteers. We then went on to Kingwood, where Bill Collins met us and told me the history of this very smart garden centre.

The estate was originally the home of the late Charles Kelley King (1867–1952), an Ohio industrialist who amassed his fortune in the early 1900's and lived at Kingwood until his death. At that time, the estate was handed over to the Kingwood Center Trust which had been developed by Mr. King. This trust made provisions for Kingwood Center to be operated as a cultural institution for the enrichment of people's lives. The trust also included an endowment which would provide the funds needed to operate the centre in years to come.

Kingwood Center was formally opened to the public in October 1953 and the buildings, gardens and grounds were altered to make for easier working and to enhance the horticultural displays. Today, Kingwood is operated as a private, non-profit making educational institution for the advancement of horticultural and other cultural activities. The emphasis is on displays of herbaceous plant material, workshops, flower shows, a horticultural reference library and public lectures. I was given a tour of this wonderful house which had eleven major rooms, ten smaller auxiliary rooms, ten bathrooms, twelve fireplaces, and was full of fine antique furniture.

The grounds consist of twenty acres of wooded property, plus a further twenty-seven acres of landscape gardens, these include a herb garden, a shade garden, perennial and rose gardens and a fine duck pond. There were trial beds which displayed some of the newest annuals as well as seven greenhouses full of flowers and plants. I was most impressed with baskets of rosemary and of tradescantia and by the overall cleanliness of the whole place. I almost forgot to mention the large collection of books and periodicals in the library and a marvellous collection of sculptured mushrooms, some 200 ceramics.

After we had looked round, I was taken to a motel where I had a bath and a short rest and was then collected by the Director and Friends of Kingwood and taken out to supper at Mokin Manor, some twenty miles away. This is an unusual place where you have your meal and are then taken on a tour of the house, which is very old. Built in 1851, it was used as a hideout for Negroes to escape from slavery.

Sunday October 18 — Bill picked me up at 8.45 am and took me to the local radio station to do a tape, after which he took me out to breakfast. I visited his home and read the Sunday papers. There was not much news about the storm, or any other English news, for that matter. We then drove back to Kingwood for a good look round. I gave my lecture at 2.00 pm, to about one hundred and fifty people (I think they liked it), and afterwards a buffet was served by the Herb Society. Most of the dishes contained herbs and it was a very tasty meal. I was also given herbs and gifts by the Society, to bring home to England. I arrived back at the hotel at 6.30 pm — nice to have an early evening. I rested on my bed, then wrote some cards to friends, and finished by writing up my diary notes.

Monday October 19 — I was picked up at Medina, halfway to Cleveland, by one of the staff from the Cleveland Garden Center. When we arrived, I was met by Jack Kerrigan who took me to Baricelli Inn, a very smart Italian hotel, and then on to lunch where I tasted my first hamburger. On then to a tour of the Rockefeller Park greenhouses and also the Cleveland Garden Center. I was told that this is one of the oldest centres in the U.S.A., founded in 1930 and is now one of the best, and is open every day. It contains Japanese and Rose gardens, herbs and perennial gardens. The library is out of this world, with over 12,500 books, ranking it as one of the largest gardening libraries in America. It also has a fine shop called "The Trellis" which is full of gifts and items from baskets to bird feeders, cards, toys and garden tools and is run by a band of dedicated volunteers. After having my hair washed and set, I went back to my hotel where Nancy, who was one of the staff, had arranged to pick me up, and together with her husband and some friends, took me to the Greenhouse, a very nice restaurant, where I had a seafood salad.

The main topic of conversation was "Black Monday" for the American people, the dollar having dropped to its lowest level in history and although this had come as a shock, apparently it had been forecast for quite a while. Nancy and I got to talking about recipes and the making of pot pourri. American ladies make lots of these, with perfumed herbs and flowers and she kindly offered to get me some oils of geranium, honeysuckle and jasmine.

It was a really interesting evening, and I went to bed at about 10.45 with a feeling of contentment.

Tuesday October 20 — Got up and had an early bath, then went down to a breakfast of melons and coffee. Muffins were served but I still can't take these early in the morning — to me they are an ingredient of a tea-time meal. I rang Jackie in England, who told me that the electricity was still off but they had tried to save some of the things in the freezer — and to think that I had left all those pies and meals for Ron to eat while I was away.

We left at nine o'clock for the Arboretum at Mentor — it's the largest arboretum in North America, consisting of several hundred acres. The magnificent gardens and flowering trees took my breath away. After our walk round, we went to lunch at Fanny's Restaurant back in Cleveland. My next thrilling visit was to one of the most distinguished American homes in Cleveland, called Gwinn. The caretaker-cum-gardener took me round and he was a very nice man. Gwinn was built in 1908 by William Gwinn Mather, an industrialist and civic leader of Cleveland. The site was chosen for its magnificent view of Lake Erie. The Renaissance balcony overlooks the lake and the Geometric Italian garden. Formal gardens to the west of the house are flanked on the north side by a charming pergola and on the southside, by a delightful teahouse with colourfully hand-painted ceilings and walls. In the centre is a pool and fountain while the greenhouses are still carefully nurtured and supply plants for both house and garden. I was most impressed with the inside of the house — some of our own royalty have stayed here. I loved the bathroom with fittings done in real gold.

As time was getting on, I went back to have a shower and change my clothes, ready for my talk. Cocktails were served at six o'clock, in the Cleveland Garden Center and afterwards a hot meal of chicken and salads, plus sweets, was served. My talk had been timed for 8.00 pm — I did sense that there were some distinguished ladies in the audience and wondered if they would be offended if I mentioned using muck in my garden at home. I enjoyed meeting the members and hoped that they appreciated my lecture on "Growing Flowers for the Flower Arranger".

Wednesday October 21 ,— Today I was not being picked up until ten o'clock — this gave me a little more time to write a few cards and finish packing, my cases are getting heavy with all the gifts which are being given to me. Joy and Bob Greer had driven from Columbus, a three-hour drive, to take me back to their home. I was to give an extra talk in Columbus which had been arranged by Rae Wright, who lives in Kettleburgh only four miles away from my home in Charsfield, in fact, she lives in my old school which has been made into a house. Joy and Bob took me to lunch at Buns in Delaware, Ohio, after which we called at W.O.S.U. radio station where I was interviewed by Tom Weible at four o'clock in the afternoon. From here we went back to Joy and Bob's home then on to the Grandview Heights Public library which is a suburb of Columbus. We arrived there at 6.00 pm, when I was to show slides of my garden. How I did that talk, I shall never know as I felt awful and was so sick — I think it must have been something I ate at lunchtime. Thankfully I managed to get through and at the end, I was given a book as a gift. So many people wanted to chat to me and although I didn't feel up to it, I was happy to talk to them. However, I was thankful to get to bed that night and was grateful to Joy, who gave me some medicine to help settle my tummy.

Thursday October 22 — Woke up feeling much better. I went round the streets this morning with Joy, who was distributing voting papers. We also visited the Nationwide Institute block, this has an elevator on the outside so I had a very good view. We went right up to the top floor, thirty-eight storeys high. At the top there are four restaurants each serving different kinds of food, dishes from England, Mexico, Ceylon and Middle America. I took lots of photos from there.

We went for lunch at a German restaurant called Gottliebs, where we met the committee members from Grandview Heights Library and afterwards visited Rae Wright's mother, who is a friend of Joy's, where we had an English tea. On the way back, we saw some lovely houses and I stopped to take pictures of them. We also saw a super pumpkin display; I have never seen so many pumpkins in one place and couldn't resist taking a photograph of these as well. At one point, I had been trying to see a pair of

Cardinals, birds a little bigger than our robins; only the male is pure red, but I was unlucky with my camera.

Had a nice rest when we got back to Joy's home and went to bed early for a change.

Friday October 23 — Left Columbus at 9.00 am; Joy and Bob drove me through the Ohio State University campus — it is massive. From there I was taken to see the Franklin Park Conservatory where there are several greenhouses and where they grow tropical plants. Apparently, many people get married in one of the large greenhouses.

Next stop — Columbus airport, where I was to catch a plane to Newark in New Jersey; this is one of the bigger airports and I stood watching planes coming in every few minutes — people seem to travel on these planes rather like we do on buses in England. I arrived at Newark Airport at twenty-past two and was met by my friends, Joan and Bob Morrison — it was lovely to see them again; they often stay in the next village to mine, when Bob comes over to England to see his publisher. As we drove to their home, the countryside was very pretty and I loved their grey and white wooden house set amongst the trees, in Morristown (the "Garden City" of New Jersey). We had a meal and sat and just talked and talked. Joan's second book, "Camelot to Kent State", all about the Vietnamese war, was just about to come out. Her first book which I enjoyed, was called "American Mosaic", written rather in the style of Ronald Blythe's "Akenfield".

Saturday October 24 — Had a good lie-in, but was up at 8.30 am and sorted out my clothes; Joan did some washing for me, that's something you hardly ever see out on the lines in the States today. One thing which I do envy, is that most homes have a very large basement where the washing can be done and hung up there to dry, well out of the way.

Later in the day I was taken for a ride around Morristown, past Washington Headquarters, and we visited Henry Wick House — this is a part of Morristown National Historical Park. New Jersey is a quiet haven of eighteenth-century America. Two centuries ago, this hilly land was the site of the 1779-80 winter encampment of some eight infantry brigades of the Continental Army during their valiant struggle in the War of Independence, with the Wick farmhouse itself being used as headquarters for Major-General Arthur St. Clair. Careful restoration of the Wick House, outbuildings, nearby gardens, orchards and open fields bring out not only these historical aspects but social and cultural features as well. In the Wick gardens, an attempt has been made, to plant not only in the spirit of the period, but wherever possible, to use varieties of plants then in existence. As my hosts and I entered Wick House, I was surprised to see two men dressed in the army uniform of the 1777 Continental Army — one was even sitting at the old table, eating a meal of that period, some sort of stew, off a tin plate and using a spoon. As I left the house and looked across the hills, it was hard to imagine five thousand men arriving at this small farm and records show how December that year introduced the worst winter of the century, to Morristown, twenty-eight blizzards blasted the hills and slopes with 6-foot snowdrifts, and bread and water was the soldier's diet — it must have been a very hard time. We got back to Joan and Bob's house at 4.00 pm and had a welcome cup of tea. I rang Ron at home and he told me that the electricity was back on — I felt better about that.

In the evening, my hosts' son and daughter-in-law came over and we went to a very smart restaurant called "The Giraffe" at Basking Ridge, just outside New Jersey. This was a celebration meal as both Joan and her son had new books just published, and they also wanted to celebrate my visit to New Jersey — we all had a wonderful evening together.

Sunday October 25 — I suppose that winter has set in now as the clocks were put back one hour last night. I was up early and wrote up my diary, then Joan took me to church in Morristown — it looked just like an English church and, funnily enough, was also called St. Peter's, the same as my church back home. I enjoyed the service and, with a choir of about seventy people, the singing was very good but, like most of our own churches, they need money for restoration.

After lunch, we visited the Macculloch Hall Historical Museum. George Perot Macculloch, a Scotsman, came to America in 1808, with his wife and two children, and in 1810 built the first-storey section of his house. In 1814, a large schoolroom was built to accommodate his Latin School for Boys and Episcopalian services were held there until St. Peter's Church was built in 1828. This red-brick federal style mansion was called the Old House by the five generations of the Macculloch's descendants who lived there continuously for one hundred and thirty-nine years. Their daughter married Jacob Welch Miller and bore nine children, the last Miller descendant to live in the house being Mrs. James Otis Post, nee Dorothea Miller. Then came the Hon. W. Parsons Todd, for many years the Mayor of Morristown — he was well-acquainted with the Miller family and familiar with the Old House. In 1949, he acquired the property, rebuilt and refurbished the mansion and gardens and opened it to the public. Very little of the original furnishings were left, but Mr. Todd had the idea that George Perot Macculloch, a cosmopolitan man, would have surrounded himself with beautiful objects. In 1976, when W. Parsons Todd died at the age of ninety-eight, the board of trustees and W. Parsons Todd Foundation set out, in his memory, a room filled with mementoes of this remarkable man. I really enjoyed walking round this house and the gardens, which the Garden Club of Morristown assists in maintaining.

Monday October 26 — My American tour is, sadly, coming to an end and today, Joan took me to Morristown Radio Station to make a tape-recording — these tapes are to be used by Radio Orwell on my return. After lunch, Joan took me out for a drive, during which I saw a whole field of pumpkins growing, with a notice saying "pick-your-own" — this reminded me of some of our fields at home, although I hasten to say that I have never seen a field of pumpkins in England. The weather has been so kind and it was really warm sitting in the car. When we returned, I stood at the kitchen window with my camera, hoping to see the Cardinal birds. These, like most birds, are very timid so I was thrilled when they put in an appearance, as I had been looking out for them during the past three weeks.

We spent a quiet evening together, just talking and it was good just to relax after all the travelling, lecturing and entertaining. Naturally, the state of the country was a topic of our conversation as this has been another "black Monday" for the American dollar — I even heard one lady describe it as "double black Monday", where will it all end, I wonder?

Tuesday October 27 — A nice day, but a sharp frost. Today was to be my first visit to the "big city" — New York. Joan's friends, Mary-Jo and Beverly, called to pick me up to take me to the English Speaking Union where I was to give my talk on "Akenfield". We left at ten o'clock and went by the George Washington bridge over the Hudson River. Along one side of the river were the Palisades, still wild and wooden, just as our Pilgrim Fathers found them. As we entered the city, I could not believe my eyes at my first sight of the tall skyscrapers. Mary-Jo parked the car and we then went to lunch at the Algonguin Hotel. This hotel is famous as the haunt of yesterday's leading American writers, who used to hold lengthy discussions here, all seated at an enormous round table (their successors probably still do). We sat next to this table — at a smaller one. After a delicious sea-food lunch we made our way to the English Speaking Union by taxi, at 16 East/69 Street. The talk went well, and after chatting with some of the audience, an English tea was served.

My friends then took me on a sight-seeing tour of the city which included a walk down Fifth Avenue and, looking in Saks Fashion Shop, I was unable to see anything in my size!! Rain was beginning to fall, and everywhere was a blaze of lights as the rush-hour had started. I was taken into Trump Towers, all done out in pink marble and brass, truly a wonderful sight but I was surprised that there were no price tags on any of the goods. As we left the building, we looked up at the Rockefeller Center, an unbelievably tall building among many very tall ones. From there, we went and visited St. Patrick's Cathedral. This lovely building looked out of place to me, in spite of the fact that the spire is 330 feet high and the interior has seating capacity for approximately two and a half thousand people. Despite its size, it was very peaceful to sit by myself here and offer a quiet prayer. I looked up at the Great Rose window, which measures 26 feet in diameter and was told that it was here that the late President John Kennedy laid in state after his assassination in 1963. The Cathedral does not appear to be busy in the way that our English Cathedrals are; I read in a leaflet that the cornerstone was laid in August 1858 and that it was formally opened in 1879. Leaving by the front door of the Cathedral, we crossed the street to look at a huge skyscraper, the Empire State Building, the world's tallest building — 1,250 feet in height; I just stood and gazed in wonder. We then walked along the street, looking at some of the most expensive shops in New York. There was so much to see and take in that my eyes became very tired. By now, it was raining very fast so we went back to the car and drove out to Joan's home, all very tired but having had another wonderful day.

Wednesday October 28 — A nice bright day after the rain last night. Today was to bring my last lecture of the tour, at the Morristown Garden Club, which was held in the church hall of the Presbyterian Church of Chatham Township. I started at two o'clock, showing slides of my garden and once again, people were very kind and came up to me afterwards, to chat and to take English tea, with some delicious cakes. Some of the committee members said that they would take me to see the Frelinghuysen Arboretum later in the week. Our drive home took us by a stream where I saw a deer drinking — it was a lovely sight. The evenings pull in now and it seems strange having tea with the curtains drawn. Having had another busy day, we decided to have a lazy evening, chatting — it's surprising how quickly the time passes, when you are with friends, and I decided to have an early night for a change.

Thursday October 29 — Up quite early, I got on with my writing then, later in the morning, went for a walk with Bob. There is so much wonderful woodland around their home and so many beautiful walks. I watched the leaves being collected by a tractor and carted away in a lorry, rather like our dustcarts. I was told that they were taken away and made into compost, which is good to know, for no bonfires are allowed. Later, I was taken out to lunch at the Spring Brook Country Golf Club and the first thing I noticed was the view from the window — it was beautiful, with a large lake and in the background, the trees all glowing with autumn colours. Once again, the food was delicious and another thing which I noticed was that, in American restaurants, water is automatically served with the food and when coffee is ordered, the waitress will soon come along and top up your cup as often as you like. We left the Golf Club, with me finishing my tenth roll of film — the views are so lovely, I do hope that the films come out well.

Friday October 30 — Another bright morning. I sorted out my suitcases, which are now so full and heavy — people have been very generous and have given me many gifts. I went along to the hairdresser later in the morning, to have my hair cut, washed and set. After lunch, we met the president of the Morristown Garden Club, Valarie Gilliland, who has been so kind and, together with some other members of the club, we went to the Freylinghuysen Arboretum; this lovely old white building looks so picturesque in the surrounding parkland. It was once the home of Matilda Freylinghuysen and on her death in 1969, the property was deeded to the county of Morris for park purposes. Converting the private estate into a public arboretum involved considerable planning. The arboretum consists of approximately 127 acres, divided into two tracts. The south tract in Morristownship has a swamp, mature forest and open fields. The north tract in Hanover township, is being developed as a demonstration area for public education and consists of rich soils along the banks of the Whippany River. I was told that there is much trouble with deer, eating and trampling down the plants. The building itself is just as fine as the grounds, and the library will certainly stay in my memory. It has a superb collection of horticultural and botanical volumes, spanning almost five centuries. I liked, and looked at, "A Curious Herbal" by Elizabeth Blackwell, 1737, and also volumes of Gerarde's Herbal, London 1636. Some of these books were given by the late Mrs. J. Cross of Morristown, and were priceless, some very small and some so large, you need a stout table to put them on!!

I was given some seeds, and a promise of help towards replacing the trees in England — what a thrilling ending to my visits to the garden centres of America.

We drove home and as Joan was getting supper ready, I stood and watched the grey squirrels eating the nuts from the bird feeder; they are very cheeky and so tame — I have seen so many of these pretty little animals and I do like them, in spite of them being vermin. Joan placed a dish of sweets by the front door as, she told me, the local children would soon be knocking for "Trick or treat", a custom for Hallowe'en Day — if you don't give a sweet, a trick will be played on you.

Saturday October 31 — This is the last day of my stay. I have had a wonderful time, have been looked after like a queen, and the kindness of all the people is something which I will never forget. Joan and I went to the big stores to have a last look round and I was surprised to see the staff all dressed in fancy costumes ready for Hallowe'en night, just as the children were yesterday (which I forgot to mention). This is something we never see in England — children in fancy dress dancing in the streets and playground. It was lovely to watch and I couldn't resist taking a photograph of them. In the stores were many fine displays of food and dish upon dish of everything you would need when arranging a party (no need to cook); every kind of salad you could think of, also sweets or desserts as the Americans call them, fresh doughnuts being made, even fresh lobster on offer.

We went back for lunch, then I sat and listened to Gardening

Questions on Radio New York. It was quite interesting, and I
rang in and asked for help with trees for Kew Gardens.

We left Morristown at 6.30 pm to go to Newark airport. On the
way, children in fancy dress were walking along with their
lanterns, hoping to get sweets and chocolates. Lanterns on
people's doorsteps also looked very pretty, with candles flickering
inside the hollowed-out pumpkins.

As I booked in at the airport, I heard a voice exclaim "There's
Peggy", and some friends from nearby Debenham were catching
the same plane home (it's a small world!). I shall think of England
as being small, after seeing this vast country. Once again, the
plane was full and hot food and drinks were soon brought round;
our watches had to be put forward, so we are now into November.

I suppose in English History, October 16th 1987, will always
be remembered, and especially so in Suffolk, for the heartbreak
which was caused by the hurricane.

The B.B.C. TV weatherman, Michael Fish, was criticised after
telling viewers just before disaster struck, that there was no
hurricane on the way. But nobody in calm old England could ever
have predicted a storm of such magnitude or destruction on such
a scale.

HINTS FOR OCTOBER

Christmas is just a few weeks away and we begin to think of Christmas plants and one of my favourites is the poinsetta, that plant with the red, pink or white bracts. Some people keep these from one year to the next and if you still have one, to make sure that the colours come again, place the plant in darkness for fourteen hours every day for approximately eight weeks starting early October — an old pedal bin liner is ideal for this purpose.

Lift and divide overcrowded herbaceous clumps, keeping the young outer growth and throwing the middle away. All border plants should be lifted and divided every third year. Remove shading from the greenhouse, checking all the glass in both them and the garden frames and making sure that the greenhouse is water-tight and that the heating is in working order. During October, late indoor flowering chrysanthemums should be brought in before any bad weather but when days are warm, try to ventilate the greenhouse whenever possible.

Remove any top growth of shoots which have flowered on roses, say one third, as this will prevent damage from rocking in the wind and generally firm bushes after gales or heavy rain. Collect up leaves which have black-spot and rust and burn them. I like to spray the bushes with Jeyes Fluid, including the soil around them (2 teaspoons to one gallon water). Tidy up the clematis — it won't hurt to clip them back if they are hanging untidily on the fence. It is quite all right to lift dahlia tubers at the end of the month and although some people like to wait until the frost has blackened the stems, I get my tubers out before the first frost or before the soil is too wet. Cut down the stem, leaving 6 to 12 inches on which to tie a label and turn upside down to dry out. Remove soil from tubers so that they dry, then dust with green sulphur to prevent mildew and place them in deep wooden boxes filled with dry peat or the material from old growbags — be sure to check frequently for rotten tubers. The same applies to tuberous begonias and gladioli, let them dry then store in dry peat. One point I would like to stress is not to cut the stems from begonias as they will part from the tuber on their own. Once my gloxinias which are growing in pots, have finished flowering, I lay them under the staging in the greenhouse to dry off completely then, next spring, start them off in heart of about 40°F or 5°C.

Strawberry runners should be planted by the end of October, to flower and fruit in two years time. It is always better to de-flower the first year as this will produce better plants.

When clearing up the garden, it is good to have a corner where you can put any hardwood cuttings because many, like flowering currant, forsythia, privet, weigela, spiraea, rosemary, blackcurrant, and roses, especially 'Queen Elizabeth', will take.

Clear up spent crops and put all leaves, etc., on the compost heap. Cover winter crops with cloches and pot up mint and parsley to put in a cool greenhouse, ready for winter use.

RED TOMATO CHUTNEY

Ingredients

1 whole head of garlic
1 piece of fresh ginger, about 2 inches long and one inch
    square
12 fl oz wine vinegar ($^3/_5$ of a pint)
2 x 14 oz tins tomatoes or 2lb fresh tomatoes, skinned
12 oz granulated sugar
$1^1/_2$ teaspoons salt
$^1/_4$ teaspoon cayenne pepper
2 tablespoons sultanas
2 tablespoons slivered almonds

Peel and chop the garlic and the ginger; put both with 4 fl oz of
the vinegar into the blender and blend until smooth. (If no
blender, chop very fine). Into a large saucepan, put the tomatoes
(including juice if tinned), vinegar, sugar, salt and cayenne
pepper. Bring to the boil and add the paste from the blender or
chopped garlic and ginger. Simmer gently for $1^1/_2$ hours until
thick enough to coat a spoon, stirring occasionally at first, then
more often as it thickens. Add the almonds and the sultanas and
simmer for another 5 minutes. Cool and bottle.

November

SUNDAY NOVEMBER 1 — Because of the difference in time, it was 10.10 am when I arrived at Gatwick airport, three-quarters of an hour late because of the fog; this was the worst part of the whole journey as the plane kept flying round and round — you knew you were home but unable to get down. On the whole though, I had a good flight with no complaints. It was wonderful to have Allan and David to meet me and as I walked through and saw them there, I realised that there is nothing like good old England and one's own folk, in fact I shed a few tears. As soon as I got into the car my sons said "Mum, you are in for a surprise but don't be too shocked when you see all the damage on the way home". As we drove along the roads, I saw so many trees down and buildings and greenhouses damaged, many beyond repair, just so much devastation. They told me that the hurricane had caused the worst disruption to services ever experienced during their lifetime. The nearer we got to Suffolk, the worse things appeared to be, and I began to almost be afraid to get home to see what damage had been done.

It was lovely to arrive home, Sally, my little dog, was over the moon and kept running round and round as though she couldn't believe that it was really me. I think that my brother Ronnie was pleased to see me home again and had even got a lunch ready for me although, if I am truthful, I was too tired to eat. The first thing I did as soon as we had eaten, was to walk round the garden to try and take in the situation. Thank God, the house had suffered no damage but the wind had moved my large wooden greenhouse from its footings and I think it will have to come down.

During the evening, my friends Iris and Claude called and it was lovely to see them. They told me how they had tried to save the things in the freezer, by taking some home and others to a friend. I realise that without their help, all the cooking and all the meals I had prepared, would have been ruined. I asked Ronnie how he had managed whilst the electricity was off and he surprised me by saying "It's amazing how you can manage on a tin of beans". Thank goodness, I had left a good stock of tinned food in the cupboard.

I still find it hard to believe all I have seen today, almost made worse by the memory of the lovely trees which I had left, in all their glory, in the United States, but we tried to get things in their right perspective by just talking to each other; however, as I was so tired, I just had to go to bed early.

Monday November 2 — I woke up, still feeling tired and still suffering from jet-lag. I just spent the morning trying to cope with the new time. I had to do some shopping at Wickham Market, then went up and collected my car from the garage where it had been for an overhaul and service. The bill came to £200, not the best thing to have happened when you have been away on a long, working holiday.

Of course, one of my first visits was to see Russell and Sarah. I took them the little gifts which I had brought back and we went out for a walk together — it was just so nice to see them again. It was David's birthday today and I had sent his card from the States, so I just rang him this morning to give him my best wishes; rather than bring him a present, I gave him some money as I know he wanted to buy something to do with his hobby, golf.

After I got back home, I'm afraid I did very little — I just went to bed early again.

Tuesday November 3 — I don't like this tired feeling as soon as I get out of bed but I suppose it will wear off before the end of the week. However, I have managed to do my E.A.D.T. article and to start sorting out the expected mountain of mail. It was just like Christmas, with a big box of letters to go through. I also did my washing, then after a quick lunch, I took a ride out to Orfordness as Ronnie had said I should go and see the woods. Going through the forests at Rendlesham, I was almost heartbroken to see the utter devastation which had been caused — this vast woodland looks as if it has suffered a wartime "saturation-bombing" raid and I don't think we shall ever see it fully restored in my lifetime. It is unbelievable what the hurricane has done. At one particular spot, at the junction of the Orford and Sudbourne roads, I took a photo of the woods looking to the left of Orford and it looked as though an aeroplane had gone right through the middle, with one side of the wood still standing while the trees on the other side had literally been snapped off about a yard from the ground. When I got home, I sorted out cuttings from the newspapers of pictures showing the effect of the hurricane, which I planned to send to my friends in America, together with the photographs which I have taken today. My phone has almost been red-hot today, with so many friends ringing to ask me all about my visit to the U.S.A.

Although I have felt able to do more today, I am still tired so had another early night.

Wednesday November 4 — Went to Radio Orwell and did my programme, "Peggy's Patch". It is quite nice to be back among friends and to see familiar faces. On my way to Ipswich I took a lot more photographs of the storm damage, the more I see, the more aggrieved I feel. I went on to see David and Norine's new home; they actually moved on the day of the hurricane. David laughed and told me that it had taken four men to hold down one small chair and get it into the lorry — it must have been an awful job. The house is very nice and it has a long garden, with a greenhouse — mind you, I wonder how much time he will spend in the greenhouse!!

From there, I went on to the W.I. group at Hardwick, near

Norwich, to give a talk and slide show, on my garden. It was five o'clock when I arrived home and I didn't do much work in the evening as, dare I say it, I still feel tired.

Thursday November 5 — The final proofs of my new book (to be called "Peggy Cole's Country Cottage Companion") arrived today. As my last corrections have to be returned as soon as possible, I only stayed a short time at the W.I. market in Woodbridge, but went on to see Iris to arrange about going through the manuscript together as we have to do it word by word; it is so important that every word and sentence is right. We decided to do it that evening. Soon after tea, Claude and Iris came over and we went through the proofs, reading a chapter each until it was finished at almost twelve o'clock. It was hard work, but I must get it back in the post tomorrow to meet the printing deadline.

Friday November 6 — First thing this morning I went to Woodbridge to get an early post for the proofs, then went on to see Allan, who showed me a video of the storm which had previously been shown on Anglia television. I then came home and made a start tidying up the big wooden greenhouse but, because of its weakened structure, I feel it is a big dodgy doing any work in there. No doubt it will have to come down eventually but I shall have to wait and see what the insurance company says. This afternoon I went to Radio Orwell and then, when I came off the air, I drove to Stowmarket to show some of my slides at a cheese and wine party; this was held in aid of the Arthritis Society.

Saturday November 7 — Woke up this morning to a miserable day which wasn't made any better because I have a heavy cold, which makes me feel a bit under the weather. Mr. Airey, who is the Robinsons greenhouse agent, called to look at my greenhouse. He told me that it was unsafe as all the glass had moved, also the wind had shifted the building off its footings. I shall now have to get another independent estimate to send off to the insurance company. Ron gave my grass a cut, and I pulled up all the bedding plants and finished tidying the borders; also sorted out the hanging baskets and took them down. I finished sending out the rest of the garden money to the various charities; in spite of the weather we have done well this year; two thousand five hundred and eighty-three pounds have been given away!

Sunday November 8 — A typical November morning, very dull as I went to the 8.30 service at Hoo Church. As this is Remembrance Day, I sat and watched as the Queen laid the poppy wreath at the Cenotaph in London; I never like this service really, as it is so sad in the way that it brings back memories of loved ones who did not survive the wars. Whilst I was watching the television, there was a newsflash telling how the I.R.A. had set off a bomb at Enniskillen in Ireland. It was awful, seven people killed and sixty injured — Poppy Day Massacre, this is what the press and broadcasters are calling it. How low can these people stoop, it seems that they have no feelings at all. Friends came around in the evening and we sat and talked, and after much debate, decided that living out here in a small village does have its advantages, though having said that, who can feel secure in any sense these days?

Monday November 9 — Back to baby-sitting today! I took Sarah and Russell into Woodbridge, they were very good, chatting all the way and telling me about how the wind had blown the trees down and smashed cars — it is surprising what they know and how much they store in their little minds. In the evening, I went to the Womens Institute A.G.M. at Charsfield; they thanked me for the coach-loads of visitors which I had sent to them for Ploughman's suppers. They had made over £200 for their funds so my visitors had helped the village in a useful way.

Tuesday November 10 — I was up early this morning and tidied up the house as at ten o'clock Mr. and Mrs. Tamping picked me up and took me to see Deborah Nunn who is still in Addenbrookes Hospital at Cambridge. She is getting so much better and I can scarcely believe what a wonderful recovery she has made so far, especially when you remember that just a few weeks back, there seemed very little hope for her. Hopefully, she will be moved to London for more treatment, at the end of the week. It was another uneventful drive back and we arrived home safely. It is rather strange that we think going to Cambridge (which is between 40 and 50 miles) is a long journey, but when I think back to my American visit, the people there will think nothing of travelling between two and three hundred miles, just to see friends or even to go out for a meal. Distances which to us appear to be to the end of the world, mean very little to them.

In the evening, I went to the Parish Council meeting at the village hall and the main topic for discussion was, inevitably, trees and re-planting.

Wednesday November 11 — The weather has turned very wet and windy today. I posted nine packets of newspaper cuttings off to friends with whom I had stayed in the States and also to various Gardening Clubs there, and then went on to do my radio programme. By 6.00 pm, the wind was blowing rather hard and I suppose that now, when gales are mentioned, we all think we are in for a hurricane again. I spent the evening making a lot of labels for my preserves and also bundled up some dried flowers ready for the W.I. market. I thought I would have an early night, just in case the wind kept me awake.

Thursday November 12 — Today was a very busy day at the Market and I quickly sold all my dried flowers, fruit and preserves. From there, I went and had lunch with Jackie and spent a very pleasant afternoon with her and the children. This evening I have been to the village of Langham, which is near Colchester, to show my slides of "Akenfield" garden, at their W.I. meeting.

Friday November 13 — Went off early to Orford, to take some

more photos, then I drove round to visit some friends at Framsden.
They told me to call in at Helmingham Park to see all the trees
which had been blown down there. I felt rather embarrassed
when I drove in the gateway and was stopped by a gracious man
— whether he was staff, family or security, I couldn't say — and
he asked me where I was going and what was my name. He told
me that I could drive in a little way, but not to go near the house.
I thought this was strange, as I was not proposing to do anything
except take a few pictures of the storm damage. But obviously I
drove further up the drive than I should have, as two gentlemen
came down to me very quickly in their car and asked me if I would
mind turning round and going out, as they had something special
on at the Hall. I noticed a lot of police cars in the background and
thought perhaps there had been a burglary but when I got home
and spoke to one of my sons, and asked what was going on, he said
"Mum, fancy you going there today, the Queen is there". I
thought, "Heavens! fancy me going there, today of all days". He
told me that Headquarters had 'phoned him to ask that I made
no mention of the incident on Radio Orwell as they didn't want
the public to know the Queen was there. However, my friends
laughed when I told them afterwards and said "Fancy trying to
take pictures of the Queen".

Saturday November 14 — We have had a busy day in the village
as it was the Over 60' s Christmas party today. We hold it earlier
now as, in the past, we have found that the older generation
won't come out if the weather is bad. Fortunately, we do not have
to worry about funds as the money which was raised from opening
my garden, will help to give them a good party. We met at the hall
at ten o'clock and set the tables; a caterer was coming in to cook
just the main course, turkey and all the trimmings and we
supplied desserts and wine etc, ourselves. It has been a nice day,
not too cold and I think the elderly guests really enjoyed
themselves. One of the nicest things about this event, is for them
to chat to one another; some of them only meet once a year at this
party. I was given a lovely flower arrangement by the rest of the

Committee, for having the garden open and supplying the funds. When I got home I felt distinctly that I am not so young as I used to be!!

Sunday November 15 — A wet day. David and Norine came over to see me for a couple of hours and they took me out for a drink at the local pub. It is a pity that they couldn't stop longer, but they were both on duty later in the day. I then got ready to have Allan, Jackie and the children for tea; I cooked a chicken and did the extra trimmings, as they had not been to have a meal with me for such a long time. After tea, I showed them slides of my trip to America — I was very pleased with my photos, they have all come out very well and I am sure that I shall get a lot of pleasure showing them at various functions. It was good to have all the family around again today; it is a pity that we cannot meet more often, but with police work and nursing shifts, this is impossible.

Monday November 16 — I tidied up the house, then got my mail off — very satisfying. I also made some quince jelly; this is a lovely jelly to have with cold meats, and I do get asked to make some of this for the W.I. market but it is not always very easy to come across quinces nowadays.

I went to look after the children and took them out for a walk as it was a nice day, after yesterday. The children helped me to take cuttings out of the newspaper as I have started to make a scrapbook of pictures to do with the hurricane. As I was away at the time, I missed a lot of the London papers but I did ask on Radio Orwell and many kind people have left me bundles of papers at reception, so I think it is going to take quite a time to get these all cut up. It is interesting to see the dramatic photos of some of the areas affected by the storm and no doubt one day this scrapbook will have historical value.

Tuesday November 17 — A really nice day, with the sun quite warm. I picked up my friend, Sheila, and together we went to

Thorndon near Eye, as I had to give a talk and show slides to the people at the Axis Club. We called in at the local pub and had a Ploughman's lunch and arrived home at half-past two. I then got the rest of the dried flowers in from my shed and made them up into bundles, then I sorted out more preserves and pickles ready to take to the W.I. market on Thursday.

Wednesday November 18 — Went off to Radio Orwell to do my "Peggy's Patch" programme. As the weather was so nice I went straight back home as I was anxious to do some work outside, tidying up the borders and cutting down the old dead flowers. I worked in the garden as long as I could before getting ready to leave at 6.00 pm for the Braintree Horticultural Club, where I was to give a talk. As I was driving along, the red light in my car came on, I was a bit worried about this so I stopped by a garage where I saw an A.A. man. He told me that the alternator was most probably on the way out but he thought it would be safe for me to carry on my journey, but to have it looked at the next day. My car seems to be costing me a lot of money these days. It is always the same; once something goes wrong, problems seem to follow each other in three's. On the car radio, I heard that there had been a terrible fire at the King's Cross Underground Station but no details have emerged yet. Having finished my talk, I managed to get home safely with no breakdown, but I did keep my fingers crossed all the way.

Thursday November 19 — The news was awful this morning and when I realised the extent of the tragedy I was shocked. The fire in London was one of the worst ever to happen in the Underground, with at least thirty-one people killed and many, many more being badly burned. You do wonder what ever is going to happen next. This has certainly been one of the worst years for accidents and indeed, as regards the weather. I took my car to the garage and they fitted a new alternator, then went on to the market at Woodbridge. This evening, I took my brother to see the doctor as a small lump had developed on his side. However, the doctor said there was nothing to worry about.

Friday November 20 — Woke up with a bad sore throat this morning, in fact, I didn't feel my usual self at all. I spent the morning writing and tidying up paper work but by the end of the day, I really began to feel down in the dumps. However, I did manage to go to Radio Orwell, but went to bed as soon as I got home.

Saturday November 21 — Although I did feel better than yesterday, I didn't get up so early today. After breakfast, I finished writing my article for the *East Anglian* and sent letters off to friends in America. I have some more slides back, from my U.S.A. trip, together with others which I had taken of the storm damage. I think the film manufacturers must have had bumper sales this year, with so many photos being taken of the storm damage, as well as the usual holiday trade.

In the paper today, I saw that the little cottage where I started my married life — Ivy Lodge, Hoo, was up for sale at £98,000; mind you, it is now two cottages knocked into one, but what a price!

Sunday November 22 — Still feeling rather unwell and not my usual robust self but as I had made an appointment to go to Christchurch Park in Ipswich at twelve o'clock, I decided to make the effort. The Park's Director was taking groups of people around to view the storm damage which the trees had sustained. It was an awful sight, with over one thousand trees being lost in Ipswich parks. Of course, I took a lot of photos while I was there. On arriving home, and after having lunch, I sorted out some more of my papers. I am still sorting out the back-log which accumulated while I was away; it is surprising how it all mounts up. I noticed signs that I have one or two mice in my shed so I cannot store apples or potatoes in there, as they will soon find them. They have even started to eat the remaining dried flowers.

After tea, Claude and Iris called round for the evening, we had a good chat and I showed them some of my recent slides.

Monday November 23 — I went over to Allan and Jackie's and took them two conifer trees which had become too big for my garden — they were delighted to have them. When I got home, I helped Ron to put the parsnips in a trench, before the bad weather begins; he is on holiday this week and is catching up on some of the jobs which need doing now. I planted all the tree seeds which I had picked up in America, and also some acorns which I found in Christchurch Park yesterday. I cleaned all the windows and then cleared my living-room as I was having a new carpet.

Tuesday November 24 — I picked up my friend, Sheila, and we went to Ipswich as we had arranged to do a little Christmas shopping together. It was not a very nice day, wet and miserable, in fact, I drove for the first time on the new Martlesham by-pass which had been opened on the nineteenth of this month. The journey is much quicker now, as you don't get delayed near Seckford Hall or in Martlesham village. When I got back, I helped Ronnie to pick up the swedes, beetroot and celeriac, as he wanted to get the land cleared ready to dig in the muck. I then went indoors, out of the rain, and peeled the Bramley apples ready for freezing.

Wednesday November 25 — Went to see friends, David Tosteven and his wife at Framsden this morning. David has been very good to me with advice about seeds and plants, so to repay him in a small way, I took him a box of apples. There was no need for me to go into Ipswich today as I had recorded my programme, so I came home and spent the rest of the day getting jams and jellies ready for the market. The easiest part, for me, is making the preserves, but it is another job getting everything labelled. The W.I. do have a high standard with the contents and labelling, as it has to be passed by a Controller each week and no shoddy or inferior goods are accepted. I am glad to be indoors as it is not very nice again today, still wet and cold.

This evening, I have been to Cotton near Stowmarket, to the V.P.A. Club, to give a talk on my garden and my personal methods of gardening and got home at about 10.30 pm.

Thursday November 26 — Made an early start to the Market; it is now beginning to get very busy, as the Christmas "rush" is starting and people are beginning to stock up for the Festive season. The craft stall is one of the nicest I have seen for many a year — there are so many talented people around, making irresistible gift-items. When I left the market, I called and had lunch with Jackie and the children. I arrived home at about two o'clock, then did a little work in the garden, cutting a lot of the roses back as they had made a lot of growth during the year. If you don't cut them back, they tend to suffer from wind-rock, where a hole appears near to the root, water fills in and when there is a frost, it can damage the root stock. I also managed to have my hair cut, by a friend in the village.

On the local radio today, there was news of a murder at Earl Soham — a lady was shot and a man badly injured, but we heard later in the day, that a woman had been questioned in connection with the incident. I spent the evening doing a lot of writing and was rather late going to bed.

Friday November 27 — I woke up this morning with one of my rotten headaches again — my late night was probably to blame. However, it eased off after I had breakfast and two or three cups of tea. I went into Woodbridge, taking Ronnie with me as he wanted to buy a small electric heater for his kitchen. We came home via Orford and Butley as it was such a nice day, and Ron showed me some of the worst storm damage around Butley, where he had been working. He also showed me where cars had been damaged when the garages had fallen in on top of them.

I went to Radio Orwell this evening, for the gardening programme and on my return, I found my friends Claude and Iris,

NOVEMBER   195

waiting for me. They had just called round on the off-chance that I would be at home, and we spent a pleasant couple of hours, chatting and sampling some of my wine.

Saturday November 28 — It was such a nice change to have a bright Saturday; Ron has been in his element carrying muck most of the day. He has done a lot of digging this week and the garden is now prepared for the winter frosts. I picked the last few flowers in the garden, also did a lot of cleaning and moving plants into the greenhouse. Afterwards, I made seven pounds of marmalade with oranges that I had in the freezer; some kind friends had managed to keep these cool when the electricity went off during the storm.

I also went up to see John Western's Exhibition of recent paintings in his little gallery at Monewden. John is a brilliant local water-colour and pencil artist; his pictures and East Anglian calendars have been in great demand now for many years. I bought two signed prints which were framed, as I thought that these would make lovely Christmas presents. In the evening, I went to look after Russell and Sarah, so that Allan and Jackie could attend the annual Police Dinner and Dance. Needless to say, I had another very late night.

Sunday November 29 — I went to the 8.30 am service at Hoo Church, then came home and did some cooking. We had the sharpest frost so far, this winter, and freezing fog, not at all pleasant. I sorted out a lot of mail, also sent off an order for seeds. I made a start on my Christmas cards, as this is quite a time-consuming job.

It was mentioned on TV today, that a journalist who had been freed from Libya, had seen Terry Waite, the Archbishop of Canterbury's Special Envoy; lets hope that this is true, it would be so wonderful if he could be home with his family for Christmas.

Monday November 30 — I thought I would have a bit of a lie-in this morning, but my little dog, Sally, thought otherwise and wanted me to get up; she won't let me rest when I might! I spent the morning sorting out different wines for the W.I. Christmas party; I usually supply this each year. I then went to Melton and took Russell and Sarah out for a little walk — we did not go as far as usual, as it was rather cold and raw outside. This evening, I have managed to do a lot more Christmas cards; the ones for America must soon be on their way, otherwise they will not arrive in time. I heard on the news today, that the U.S. dollar was the lowest since the Second World War — the American people must be very worried indeed.

I also heard the sad news today, that Irene Handel had died. I always liked this fine actress and comedienne; she was very talented and had given much pleasure to many people.

November has also seen the death of another famous broadcaster, Eamonn Andrews; he will be especially remembered, of course, for his long-running programme "This is Your Life".

HINTS FOR NOVEMBER

Sow broad beans, Aquadulce, Claudia, or The Sutton, in the middle of November, in rows 18 inches apart and planting seeds at 6–8 inch intervals.

Why not plant up a hanging basket with pansies, bellis double daisies, polyanthus, arabis, alyssum and saxatile also miniature daffodils and narcissi and anemones, using a good multi-purpose compost which now contains a special water-holding substance. Start amaryllis (hippeastrum) off if you have an old plant. If, however, you have a new one, plant the bulb half showing above the compost in bottom heat (min. 60°F/15°C). Water sparingly until flower begins to open then also start to give a feed.

Lift and store carrots and beetroots in dry clean sand or, again, I have used the contents of old growbags. My brother lifts parsnips and a few leeks and makes a trench near the path in which to put these vegetables. They are then covered with soil so that when bad weather sets in, all we need to do is to pull the parsnip or leek from the trench and this saves standing on wet soil or frosted ground.

Lift a clump of rhubarb and leave on top of the ground to get well frosted, then move it into the greenhouse and place under staging in a deep wooden box of leaf mould or soil-less compost — you should then get some very early pink sticks of tasty rhubarb.

Another old saying "Set trees at All Hallowtide (2nd November) and command them to grow; set them after Candlemas (2nd February) and entreat them to grow", so you can understand why we say plant trees and shrubs in late autumn. Soil temperatures are still warm and autumn rains are helpful. Good preparation is very important so add plenty of good rolled manure to the soil when planting the tree or shrub and also put a good stake in the hole first, then firm the tree to the stake.

Prune apple trees which have produced upright growing leaders, pruning to an outward-facing bud, but those with a relaxed spreading habit should be cut to an inward-facing bud. Pear trees — cut back to within a few inches of their bases and shorten leaders by about one third; thin out old unfruitful spurs.

If you have clumps of agapanthus, they will need protection in cold areas so place straw or bracken over the crowns. Hydrangeas may also need some protection. Please don't cut old flower heads off and these will help to protect the tender flower buds which will produce next year's blooms. Protect Christmas roses (helleborus niger) from rain and mud splashes during the winter, by covering them with a piece of glass, suitably supported.

The seed catalogues will be coming through the letterbox so do make sure that you get your order off at the earliest opportunity or your favourite varieties will be sold out!

PEAR, DATE & NUT CHUTNEY

Ingredients

3lb pears
4oz seedless raisins
4oz stoned dates
8oz walnut halves
8oz brown sugar
Juice of 3 lemons
2 teaspoons salt
$^1/_2$ pint wine vinegar or white vinegar

Peel, core and chop the pears, chop the raisins, dates and walnuts.
Place all the ingredients in a preserving pan and bring to the boil,
stirring until the sugar is dissolved. Simmer gently until tender
and the desired consistency is reached.
    Pour into warm jars, cover and seal.

December

TUESDAY DECEMBER 1 — Went to Wickham Market to get my post off for the U.S.A. — it is surprising how expensive it can become, but I had got some nice photos and cuttings, so I was pleased to get them all packed off.

I came home and checked around the garden; even at this late time of the year, there are still many berries on the bushes. My rose, Rosa Rubrifolia is absolutely full of berries. I managed to get my *East Anglian* article finished, then had the rest of the day tidying up the house.

Wednesday December 2 — Off to Ipswich to do the radio programme, in pouring rain. I didn't stay in Ipswich long as I wanted to sort out more jams and pickles for the W.I. market tomorrow; the times I have wished that I had a bigger cupboard to keep all these packed away.

I bet there are not many people who have boxes of preserves stacked all around their bedroom.

At last, the lectures have died down for a spell and, in a way, it is quite a relief to be able to stay in at night.

Thursday December 3 — Went to the market this morning and called on Jackie and the children before going to Ipswich to show slides at Tower House; this was in aid of M.I.N.D. The people helped by this organisation are those who have suffered breakdowns in their lives, and when you see some of these pour souls, it does make you appreciate your own good health. They enjoyed the slides and I was pleased to be able to have lunch with them and to chat with some of them. I got home from Ipswich at half-past three.

This afternoon, I saw Margaret and Richard Kitson, these are the farmers who live opposite, and they told me that I could rent a piece of their field for car-parking, when we have the garden open; this is wonderful news as it will help our parking problem enormously. My brother will be so pleased to hear this!

Friday December 4 — I received the proofs of my book this morning, so I sat and had two hours going through them. I must say that it is beginning to look very good and I believe that the end result will be acceptable. I have only scanned the proofs as I have a lot of cakes to make today before I am able to go to Ipswich to do the usual gardening programme. Returning home from Ipswich, I had quite a late night, actually reading through the book.

Saturday December 5 — Not a very nice day. I watched the last straw bales being carried off the field opposite, it is the first time that I can remember seeing bales out on the fields so late in the year. Later this morning, I went to Ipswich to open a Christmas Bazaar, then came back to Melton as it was Russell's birthday party. This is the first time that he has had a party with his own little friends. It seems such a pity that they grow up so soon, so it is lovely to enjoy the moments of happiness while they are still small.

This evening, I had another go at reading the proofs, this seems to be a time-consuming job and it was nearly midnight before I put them down.

Sunday December 6 — As there was no early service today at Hoo, I got up and finished reading the proofs — thank goodness, I have now come to the end. I then cooked lunch and afterwards, as the weather had turned a little brighter I spent the afternoon cleaning windows in the metal greenhouse. This took some time and I was glad to sit down at night. Iris and Claude came round this evening and helped me to sort out picture captions for Alfred Geary's beautiful line drawings which are to be used in my book.

Monday December 7 — I got up, and making an early start outdoors, gave my greenhouse a good wash with Jeyes Fluid. I also moved my dahlia tubers into the wine shed, first making sure that they were dry and well wrapped up. Everything in the garden is at the dormant stage now, so it is just a matter of tidying things up and making sure that no harm will come to them through the cold winter months. I worked outside until it began to get dark, then went indoors and had an early tea as I was going out later in the evening to baby-sit for Allan and Jackie over at Melton. When I came home in the early hours of the morning, I found that the night air was very cold and because of the sharp frost, I had quite a problem getting the ice off the car, before I was able to drive home.

Tuesday December 8 — Went to Ipswich today and bought a second-hand wall unit and bookcase which I had seen advertised in the paper. It was a nice strong one — my sons laughed and told me that it was as well, as it would soon be filled up with books and papers. On the way back, I called and had coffee with David and Norine, then came home and wrote a lot of notes for "Peggy's Patch" programme tomorrow. I had started to do some work in the wine shed when a representative from Robinsons Greenhouses called; we talked for some time before I finally made up my mind to order a new greenhouse from them. After looking at so many different models, I feel that the one which I have chosen is probably the strongest and most suitable for my needs even though it is a little more expensive than some of the others. This evening, I have felt quite tired after all my exertions, so I decided to go to bed early.

Wednesday December 9 — Off to Ipswich early this morning, where first of all I dropped off my seed list at Thompson and Morgan (What a boon it is to have this famous seed specialist firm so near and handy!) Then I called in to see Peter and Jean Woods, on the Camden Road, and they gave me several large pots of pelargoniums. Next — and most important of today's jobs — I posted off my final proofs to David & Charles, the publishers, after which it was back home and down to earth again, sorting out more dried flowers for tomorrow's market. It is remarkable how effective these look when just a few are put with wild grasses; wild oats especially look very pretty, with two or three contrasting flower-heads. I experiment a lot with many different blooms, hanging them up to see which will dry suitably, that is, without losing their shape or colour.

Thursday December 10 — Off to Woodbridge, anticipating another very busy morning at the W.I. market, as the festive season approaches; thirty pounds of marmalade were sold in ten minutes — this was not all mine, I may add, but we do find that people are keener than ever to buy home-made preserves these days. Queues of people were waiting for the doors to open. I did a little shopping in Woodbridge, then came home and selected some suitable wines ready for the local W.I. party which is to be held this weekend. I had already got some out but it is surprising how long it takes to do this job properly and balance up the sweet and dry varieties. However, it is quite a pleasant job, although trying the different sorts can make you end up feeling rather tipsy!!

Friday December 11 — My neighbour, Mr. Spicer, called round this morning to see whether I would like to pick some plums to make into wine. It was quite a sight to see them so late in the year, hanging on the trees, that I came home and got my camera to record the event. I don't know how the wine will turn out, whether it will have too much acid or not enough tannin, but anyway, I shall try a gallon just to see. By two o'clock, it was pouring with rain so there was very little else I could do outside today. I went off to the radio station in the late afternoon, then spent time on my return, going through a lot of my books. People pull my leg and say that my house must be the "Charsfield Library", but I do turn to them so often for reference for the articles which I write.

Saturday December 12 — I got up at 5.00 am, rushed through some chores, then went to Radio Orwell as it was their "Operation Santa Claus" Day. Money is raised by selling goods and bids are given over the phone, so they needed extra people to answer the telephones and to help in the studio. I stayed until eleven o'clock and then came home and potted up some herbaceous plants, which I had previously split up. Ronnie dug a trench for me, ready to lay the electricity cable underground, in preparation for my new greenhouse. I later cleaned all my brass and trophies, an easy job which I can sit and do when my mind is on other matters. My bookcase and unit came today, it goes well in my sitting-room and is much more stable than my old one.

Sunday December 13 — I went to Hoo Church this morning for the early service, then cooked lunch and tidied up my desk. Some friends from Ipswich called in during the evening, but I did manage to make further progress with my Christmas cards before they arrived. Every year I say I will get this seasonal task done early, but it never works out that way!.

Monday December 14 — Was up early again to finish preparing the wine for the W.I. party — bottles of apple, grape, sloe, blackberry and cherry (I've no doubt that this will bring a glow to their cheeks later this evening).

Little Russell had his party at Playschool today, so I took Sarah to see the little ones singing their carols. I got home here at five o'clock, changed, then went off to the Village Hall. We had a very good meal — soup, cold turkey, ham and salads, sherry trifle, coffee and mince pies, all washed down with the wine. The evening was a very pleasant one and by the many expressions of thanks, everyone enjoyed themselves.

Tuesday December 15 — Those Christmas cards are still not completed, so I made them my first job. I then baked mince pies and cakes and put the marzipan on my Christmas cake. Whilst I was doing this, some friends called to get some holly to decorate Melton Church. Sadly there were no berries on it but I do have quite a lot of the variegated kind. This afternoon, I went to make a start on the decorations in Charsfield Church, as the children hold their Christingle service tomorrow night.

It was a busy day, one way and another, and I can see that it will be all go, on every front, now that the festive season is getting into full swing.

Wednesday December 16 — Not a very nice day, pouring with rain. I went off to Ipswich, did my usual programme, then went and bought some flowers so that I could finish off decorating the pedestal in the church. When I got home from the church, I weighed up some apples, leeks, parsley and swiss chard, ready to take to tomorrow's market. The rest of the day was spent doing labels for my pickles and preserves, again for the market. Then some more Christmas cards, some with letters.

Thursday December 17 — Set off to the market, heavily loaded up this morning as this was to be the last one for 1987. We had a very busy session and over one thousand pounds was taken in one hour!! By eleven o'clock, it was absolutely pouring with rain but despite this inconvenience, I went and bought a lot of stamps from the Post Office, for my cards. I have now written over one hundred and fifty cards — the list just gets longer every year! Having made sure of my stamps, I drove out to the Coach and Horses at Melton, to join the members of Woodbridge W.I. for our annual lunch. This was very enjoyable and I arrived home at 2.30 pm — to catch up with a lot of housework and generally tire myself out by bedtime.

Friday December 18 — I think I have actually finished my cards, at least I hope so. The weather is certainly much milder today. I had my cockerels, for Christmas, from a local farmer this year, deciding to have a change from turkeys, and these were delivered this morning. They weighed twelve pounds each, lovely big birds; as well as my own, I bought one each for the boys and their families. I dressed them and put them into the freezer.

I managed to find a little white kitten as a present for my friends at Framsden; they had been looking for one for such a long time, so I was quite pleased. I then sorted out my vegetables which were in store, checking over the carrots and beetroot to make sure that they were alright, after which I travelled to Ipswich for the gardening programme on Radio Orwell.

Saturday December 19 — Went off to Woodbridge early as I had bought the wrong plastic fixings for putting up my bubble polythene in the greenhouse. On the way back, I called in at the church to put the finishing touches to the Christmas decorations. In the afternoon, as the weather was so mild and there were no fish in them, I cleaned out my ponds. Being in the mood for cleaning, I decided to clean out the chicken hut. As it was still light, I planted my Christmas tree in a tub and brought it indoors. After tea, I started to put up the decorations round the sitting room, with Ronnie's help, bless him! Later on, we went with some friends to a Christmas party at Monewden, I took some bottles of home-made wine with me and, all in all, it was a very jolly evening.

Sunday December 20 — The weather is still very mild, not at all like Christmas weather. I just hope that we don't have to suffer for it in the New Year. I went to the 8.30 service at Hoo Church, then after an early lunch, I started to move plants around in my cold greenhouse. As my friend, Perry, is going to have my old wooden greenhouse, I have to transfer some plants from there. The radio forecast talks about the temperature becoming colder this coming week, although it doesn't seem much like it at the moment. Ronnie finished cleaning out my ponds while I had to draw and dress six chickens for friends. I also killed two of mine, as I have five cockerels running around and they had started to fight amongst themselves.

Monday December 21 — Went to Framlingham early this morning and took a present to my sister, Eileen, together with some vegetables and apples, then called on some old neighbours who had moved to Framlingham, and had coffee with them.

I then went on to see Jackie, taking her chicken and bits and pieces, ready for her to use for Christmas. Allan washed my car while I was there, this was a nice bonus for me as it is not one of my favourite jobs. I called at a local store on the way home and bought sticks of brussels sprouts and some swedes, as I am getting short of vegetables in the garden now. As sprouts are only twenty pence for a stick, they are quite good value.

We had our neighbours in for the evening and quite honestly, I was glad of the excuse to sit down and have a rest. We had a very pleasant time, "sampling" the home-made wine!

Tuesday December 22 — According to my diary, winter begins today and this is the shortest day of the year; we shall have to wait and see what the weather outlook is likely to be in the long-term. My publisher rang and I had a long chat with him about my book; everything seems to be going very well. I went down to Hoo Church and did a window arrangement, they are so short of people now in Hoo, that I have been asked if I can help out with the annual decorations.

David and Norine came over, as well as Iris and Claude, so we all decided to go up to the local pub for lunch. When I arrived home, my friend John came over and moved the electric wire from my old greenhouse into the smaller one where all my plants are now housed; at least I shall have heat there if the weather does get bad. Looking around, I can hardly believe that I have crammed all my plants into this one small greenhouse. Soon after, David and Norine left with a "Red Cross Parcel", as he calls it — chicken, preserves, cakes, mince pies and so on.

Wednesday December 23 — The weather is still very mild. I went to Ipswich today for my "Peggy's Patch" programme but there were so many people in town, I was really glad to get home. I tidied up the wine shed and sorted out the wine for Christmas gifts; I also did some tidying up in the conservatory. This evening, I iced my Christmas cake and plucked and dressed two more cockerels, then I strained my sloe gin. It was an ideal job for the end of the day as I was able to sample the brew — then go to bed!

Thursday December 24 — I went out early and had my hair trimmed and set, called on Jackie with brussels sprouts and parsnips, then went on to Ipswich as Radio Orwell were giving each presenter a turkey. The traffic was simply awful; I left home at nine o'clock and didn't get back until one — anybody would think that the shops were going to be closed for a month. It is terrible to think that so many people in other parts of the world are starving, and we are absolutely going over the top with food here. Ronnie finished work early so he came and did some clearing up around the rose beds; all the digging is done now. I made two holly wreaths and took them up to the church to put on Ernie's and Mum and Dad's graves. How my Ernie would have loved to have seen the grandchildren — they are so excited at the thought of Christmas and really the season has most meaning when seen through the eyes of little children. I feel so sorry for people on their own at Christmas, it hits them very hard. While I was out, I delivered some bottles of wine to the Vicarage and to the garage, as well as to the neighbours along the row. I also made some mulled wine to take to the church as it was decided this year, to give each person a glass before they leave the late-night service on Christmas Eve. I went to the Midnight Christmas Service and got home at a quarter to one.

Friday December 25 — A lovely, mild Christmas morning; I went to the 8.30 service at Hoo Church and the sun was shining quite warmly through the windows. I got home and waited for

Ronnie to come down, then we went over to Allan and Jackie's to spend Christmas Day with them. We had a very nice day, it was lovely to see the children's faces when they discovered their presents. David and Norine were at work so we couldn't be all together as a family. Ronnie and I got back to Charsfield at eleven o'clock.

Saturday December 26 — Was up at the usual time but had a lazy day; it was nice just to be able to relax. After I got lunch (although we didn't feel like eating much), I went up and fiddled about in my potting shed. Ronnie did some sorting out in the shed; we both found it a job to try and relax, but it was nice just fiddling about outside in the warm, mild weather. I took Sally for a good long walk round the village and in the evening, just sat and began marking up my new diary, then watched television.

Sunday December 27 — Had an unusual speaking engagement today. The manager of the Crown Hotel at Woodbridge thought it would be a nice idea to have a local person give an illustrated talk to his Christmas holiday guests, before they departed, so I was asked to talk for about an hour and show some of my slides of the "Akenfield" garden. The talk went well and a number of the guests expressed their interest and enjoyment afterwards.

My friends, the Rowe's, came over from Stowmarket and we had a pleasant lunch together at the hotel.

An amazing number of people were out walking in Woodbridge today, in the bright warm weather; I was glad that I wore a light-weight suit and could leave my coat in the car.

At home in the evening, I wrote up my gardening notes, to round off another enjoyable day.

Monday December 28 — The weather is still very mild — I woke up so warm in bed that I had to take off some of the covers; just imagine that at the end of December! Some parts of the country today had temperatures up in the sixties. Ron and Eric (Perry's husband), started taking down the old wooden greenhouse and, in spite of the hurricane, it came down very well. Eric took all the glass home on a tractor and trailer, then came back for the frame. They were very lucky, only cracking one pane of glass during the whole operation.

We had rather a sad accident happen at Charsfield Hall yesterday, when a young boy was killed there; he was only four years old. A piece of spraying equipment had fallen on to him when he was playing in an old barn, together with some other children.

Tuesday December 29 — Had a rotten headache all day, so didn't feel very energetic but spent the morning writing letters and thank-you notes; at least I have caught up with some of my mail. I moved a lot of wine round to make room for more, perhaps we must start drinking more. The weather is still very mild — it doesn't seem at all natural. In the evening, I went to look after Russell and Sarah, while their parents were out and got home at midnight.

Wednesday December 30 — I went to Ipswich for the radio programme, called on some friends afterwards, then came home and did my article for the Women's Institute newspaper. After tea, I had my neighbours David and Pam Peck and their daughters in, and we had a drink to toast the New Year; a bit early but it was nice to have them round. I also showed them a selection of slides from my trip to America, which they obviously enjoyed.

Thursday December 31 — What a day to finish the old year! The bright warm weather was the first topic of conversation here with everyone, and I should think that it will go down in history as some sort of record.

Nineteen eighty seven will certainly stay in my mind for the wonderful trip I made to the U.S.A., for the generosity of my hosts and for the many delightful friends I made out there. But no doubt, others here at home will long recall the hail in August, the hurricane in October (which I missed!) and the many gales we had during the year.

I went into Woodbridge to do some shopping as the family are all coming over for the day tomorrow. When I got home, I stuffed my 'Radio Orwell' turkey and put out some special vegetables for the occasion.

The garden has been a joy to us all again this year, despite the often uncertain weather; Nature has a wonderful way of "getting to the church on time", I always think! We also had a good year for visitors and I was able to hand over more than two and a half thousand pounds to national and local charities.

In so many ways, I have a lot for which to be thankful.

HINTS FOR DECEMBER

DECEMBER takes away everything and returns nothing. Perhaps it is the short days and cloudy skies of this month which make it all seem so dismal. However, we have Christmas preparations to think about and churches to be decorated. This is where our dried poppy seed heads, honesty (which look like mother-of-pearl moons) and chinese lanterns come into their own. Montbretia or crocosmia seed heads dried and sprayed with gold or silver paint, can be used — these look very attractive amongst the holly and ivy; I was always giving hints and advice, on the radio programme, about cutting holly and other greenery. Don't just cut the shrub haphazardly as it will soon spoil the shape. Briza maxima (quaking grass) and many other dried flowers can be used, which are extremely decorative.

I have often been asked how to plant mistletoe — you will need to keep berries from March to May. These are semi-parasitic and some people simply squash them on the underside of a branch of apple, hawthorn, poplar or mountain ash; this is fine if the birds leave them alone. Others may make a v-shaped cut, raise the bark and slip the seed inside. Growth is slow at first but, once a leaf shows, the plant grows quickly and often tends to break out in different places on the tree.

As you walk around the garden, check wall shrubs and climbers for loose ties and shoots and secure against strong winds and possible bad weather. If we do get snow make sure that you shake the branches to remove it to avoid damage which can soon spoil the look of a plant and allow diseases to enter the wood. This is a good time to wash pots and trays — soak them in an old tin bath of water to which Jeyes Fluid has been added. Garden labels can also be cleaned and give garden tools a good clean and wipe with an oily rag.

Shallots are one of the first vegetables to start for the new season and custom dictates planting on the shortest day and harvesting on the longest. Another job which I like to do on Boxing Day, is to plant onion seed in the greenhouse. This needs good soil and heat, sixty to sixty-five degrees Fahrenheit, to get it to germinate. Prick out as soon as it can be handled, about the size of a darning-needle.

Check garden pools to make sure that you have something like empty washing-up containers or tennis balls, floating on the surface, if you have fish in the pond. I know that it doesn't look very attractive but it helps to stop ice forming and the fish can get some air.

Many people will have been given cyclamen and poinsettias as the two most likely flowering presents, at Christmas. Cyclamen will soon die if over-watered, so wait until it shows signs of asking for water — it doesn't sound a very kind way to treat a plant but it will last much longer; don't stand it in a hot room, 50 to 55°F is ideal. Poinsettias, on the other hand, like warmth, up to 70°F; again do not over-water but wait to see the compost dry out.

DELUXE MINCEMEAT PUFFS

Ingredients
Ground Almond flaky pastry   Pinch of salt
10oz plain flour   12oz butter
4oz ground almonds   1 tablespoon lemon juice
2oz ground rice   6 tablespoons iced water

Make up as for flaky pastry. Roll out the cold pastry and cut into 4in squares. Place 1 tablespoon mincemeat on each square and fold over diagonally, sealing joint with beaten egg. Brush the top with egg and sprinkle with a little demerara sugar. Place on a baking tray and bake in the middle of a hot oven Gas 7 or 425°F, for 12 to 15 minutes until risen and golden brown.

Serve with rich brandy butter.